FRENCH VEGETARIAN COOKING

Simply delicious recipes for every occasion, from healthy snacks to gourmet meals — all with that special French magic!

Ex Libris

Edna Collie

By the same authors
CUISINE VÉGÉTARIENNE FRANÇAISE
FRENCH FISH CUISINE

French VEGETARIAN COOKING

Jean Conil and Fay Franklin

THORSONS PUBLISHING GROUP
Wellingborough, Northamptonshire
•
Rochester, Vermont

First published 1987

© JEAN CONIL and FAY FRANKLIN 1987

British Library Cataloguing in Publication Data

Conil, Jean
French vegetarian cooking.
1. Cookery, French 2. Cookery, (Vegetables)
I. Title II. Franklin, Fay
641.6'5'0944   TX719

ISBN 0-7225-1263-5

Printed and bound in Great Britain by
Hazell Watson & Viney Limited,
Member of the BPCC Group,
Aylesbury, Bucks

Contents

Introduction

When the initial announcements were made of our first book on the subject of French vegetarian cooking, *Cuisine Végétarienne Française*, they were greeted with one or other of two very distinct reactions.

The first was derision! How could one possibly equate two subjects so diametrically opposed to one another? How could one marry great French cuisine to humble vegetarian cooking? After all, surely we could see that the French love their meat so much that there could be nothing in the cuisine of that country that would be acceptable to a vegetarian? The idea was preposterous — it would never work. Or so we were told, and by some very genuine Francophiles. Even by some vegetarians. Certainly by several top professionals.

The second reaction was one of delight, and of amazement that such a book had not already been written. For any food-loving vegetarian who has ever travelled in France is already aware of the wealth of good food available to them, in both shops and restaurants. Discounting, of course, the more traditional charcuteries and the horse butchers, there is to be found in French shops all manner of delights for the gourmet that have nothing to do with meat, poultry or fish. Meat-eaters are often not even aware when selecting their food that many of the items they have chosen — the *tarte à l'oignon*, the *champignons à la grecque*, and so forth — that these dishes are fundamentally vegetarian in origin. The vegetarian is acutely, and pleasantly, aware.

And any lover of good food, vegetarian or omnivore, will eulogize on the French respect for the vegetable. Not here the overcooked, overlooked pile of greyish-green at the side of the plate. Always, but especially in recent years, the French chef has seen the vegetables served as an asset, albeit an adjunct, to a great meal. They are prepared with care and attention, cooked to perfection, dressed with respect for their colour and flavour, served with style. They are chosen judiciously when animal protein is prepared, too, for any chef worth his *toque* knows that it is the vegetable that makes the dish. A plain sautéd steak is protein and nourishment, but a steak *chasseur* is cuisine. And the difference? Why, mushrooms, tomatoes and (of course) a little wine! Don't forget, either, that the diamond of the French kitchen — which adds a magical charisma to the finest cooking — is that elusive little subterranean cousin of the mushroom, the truffle.

The country people have just as high a regard for vegetables, however, as the greatest of chefs. For them, the centuries have gleaned a harvest of substantial, nourishing food that owes little to animal produce. Grains, fresh vegetables, fruits — all these play a vital part in traditional French country cooking, from the *choucroute* of the North to the *ratatouille* of Provence. Where animal protein has a role to play, it is more likely to feature as dairy produce or eggs. And success in what French dish is more striven after by most apprentice cooks than the charming and simple cheese soufflé?

No wonder, then, that true lovers of French cuisine welcomed a book that aimed to gather a collection of French vegetarian recipes from both the formal and the country kitchen. And no wonder that *Jean Conil's Cuisine Végétarienne Française* has done so well. But it was plain to see that such a book could but scratch the surface of the genre. Much was included, but much omitted. The very finest of recipes, too, often meant dishes for formal dinners, with ingredients lists and prices that precluded their use for everyday cooking. To win hearts and minds, we had to dazzle — and dazzle we did, with feasts for the mind, the eye and the palate.

But it was clear that a need still existed — or perhaps had been created? That need was for a collection of simpler recipes that could be absorbed into the family repertoire of favourite meals. While such dishes had been included in the first book, the wealth available certainly had been scarcely tapped. And, from talking to people and hearing their needs, there was perhaps an emphasis yet to be fully stressed. Since the publication of the first book, the revolution in public awareness of food has reached new peaks. A book listing the true meanings of the additives in our processed foods, *E for Additives* by Maurice Hanssen, has reached the top of the British bestseller charts. Supermarkets and manufacturers have begun to advertise their food as low-fat, or additive-free, or high-fibre. There has been an increased demand, perhaps as a result, for food that was as quick and simple to prepare as the 'old' sort, and that tasted and looked as appealing (especially to children), and that was as economical. A hard list of criteria to meet, indeed!

But meet it we have to, if we value the health of our children, and of ourselves, and of our nation. In a busy world, who has time to prepare elaborate dishes for everyday food? Simple and good food is available, but if recipes are not forthcoming which put it to good use swiftly, or sensibly, then the result might perhaps be apathy, and a swing back to the junk food of the past.

So the emphasis of this book has been to take the natural French love of food, and love of economy, and inborn sense of 'time-and-motion' to choose dishes that reflect these virtues and that will be enjoyed by all the family. We have given much thought to people on the move — children at school, mother and father at the office, and so forth, in assembling many dishes that pack protein, vitamins, minerals, fibre and energy into easy-to-carry, easy-to-eat, delicious form. Good things truly do come in small parcels, in this respect!

We have looked to recipes that can be prepared in advance, either for family suppers or for entertaining family, friends or colleagues at the end of a hard-working day. Just as the previous book included some simple country dishes we have, to balance things out, presented in these pages some special treats that involve more time, more effort, and a little more cash — that is a natural French urge to highlight *la différence,* with which we trust you will concur.

We have, as usual, striven to use natural, whole foods. To choose dried fruit and honey as sweeteners, to use whole grains and flours, to select dishes that balance proteins without the over-reliance on high-fat produce. For the last reason we have placed considerable importance on the use of the wonderful Oriental food tofu, or *fromage de soya* as we call it. We do not pretend that its use is traditional in French cuisine, although we are adopting it with great enthusiasm now that it has reached us via the fashionable and exquisite Vietnamese cuisine that has taken France by storm of recent times. But then, no one is saying that wholefoods are always used in traditional French recipes. In the past, white flour and other refined products were sought out as being 'better' than brown, because they indicated greater wealth or higher social standing. Now, making such substitutes is valid in light of our greater understanding of what is good for us.

Equally, we accept that, where meat was available, it would have gone into the pot — and into the recipe. Bones would have been part of the basis for stock; a scattering of fat bacon would have garnished some vegetable dishes if to hand; lard or dripping would have sautéd others, or greased a dish, at the start of a casserole or pie. We make no apologies for replacing such items with their vegetable equivalent. If a dish is so weak that a taste of meat is needed to make it work, then it is not good enough for inclusion in this book. Everything here stands up to discerning tastes on its own merits and is derived from a recipe that was, essentially, vegetarian.

The use of tofu means that more dishes than in my previous books are suitable for vegans. A vegan diet is a radical idea in France, there is no doubt. But we know from talking to those at the forefront of medical health research that the old ideas about veganism are disappearing just as have those about vegetarianism over the past few years. It is an area which deserves considerable time and research, and we hope that the recipes in this book that are suitable for vegans will mark the beginning of a more considered approach to this diet on the part of the professional chef.

Now we come to the recipes themselves. As always, we have tried to come up with something for everyone. As always, we have included just a sample of the breathtaking scope we know to be available to the imaginative cook, and we invite you to look upon these pages as a fund not only of recipes but also of ideas. We have been overjoyed by the response to the idea of French vegetarian cooking, and we trust that the enthusiasm that we feel, and that has been shown to us by others, for this culinary movement will be shared by everyone who uses this book.

À votre santé!

Chapter 1
LES SOUPES POTAGÈRES

Soups from the Garden

A soup or *potage* is more often than not a meal in itself, as far as the French are concerned. The real peasants, like myself, like to soak bread in their soup — a style known as *mitonnage* or *tremper la soupe*. This is usually done just before the soup is served. The cook places slices of bread (often stale) in the tureen and then pours the soup or broth over them. After a couple of minutes the soup is placed on the table for everyone to enjoy, complete with morsels of melting country bread that thickens the soup and satisfies even the hungriest of appetites.

These home-made soups are part of everyday life in France. They are so simple and cheap to make, and so good to eat, that I am always amazed by the market for tins and packets that thrives in most countries. Nothing whets the appetite as much as the aroma of a rich vegetable soup simmering on the stove, and very little need go to waste in the kitchen if a pot of stock is there in preparation for tomorrow's dinner.

In the region of Amiens the marshlands have been turned over to vegetable cultivation, and it is from there that we get the *primeurs* — the baby carrots, turnips, radishes, leeks and so forth — that flourish early in the rich humus of the marsh. The fields are divided by canals, and the gardeners go about in boats called *cornets* to gather their produce. This type of cultivation is called *hortillonnage* and is thought to have been developed by the Romans during their occupation of France. A soup made from the tender vegetables of that region is a unique gastronomic experience, but such pleasure can be recreated by the caring cook with produce from the garden or the market.

You will find in this chapter just a selection of soups from the French countryside, all of which will add savour to your table in a way that only good home cooking can. All would make a splendid lunch or supper, served with a chunk of good crusty bread and perhaps a glass of cider or *vin de pays* — a simple meal, the enjoyment of which could scarcely be equalled by the finest restaurants in the land.

VELOUTÉ DE POIS VERTS À LA MENTHE

Chilled Pea Soup with Mint

Serves: 6
Preparation time: 15 minutes
Cooking time: 45 minutes, plus chilling time

In the region of Clamart, not far from Paris, are grown the most delicious petits pois — as sweet as honey and exquisitely tender. This chilled soup is an ideal use for the first fresh peas of the Summer.

Imperial (Metric)	American
1 small soft lettuce heart	1 small soft lettuce heart
2 lb (900g) fresh green peas	2 pounds fresh green peas
2 tablespoons peanut oil	2 tablespoons peanut oil
1 small onion, finely chopped	1 small onion, finely chopped
1 shallot, finely chopped	1 shallot, finely chopped
1½ pints (850ml) boiling water	3¾ cups boiling water
2 oz (50g) blanched almonds	⅓ cup blanched almonds
3 fl oz (90ml) hot water	⅓ cup hot water
5 leaves fresh mint	5 leaves fresh mint
Sea salt	Sea salt
Freshly ground black pepper	Freshly ground black pepper
Toasted flaked almonds to garnish	Toasted slivered almonds to garnish

Separate the lettuce leaves, wash thoroughly and drain. Shell the peas.

Heat the peanut oil in a large pan and sauté the onion and shallot until translucent.

Shred the lettuce leaves and add to the pan, along with the peas. Sauté for 5 minutes, then stir in the boiling water, cover and simmer for 35 minutes.

Place the blanched almonds in a blender goblet with the hot water and purée to a smooth cream. Pour into a bowl and reserve.

Pour the cooked soup into the blender and purée, along with 2 leaves of mint. Add this mixture to the bowl and stir to blend in the almond cream. Cover and chill.

Before serving, season to taste. Serve sprinkled with chopped mint and toasted almonds.

VELOUTÉ DOUX DE CONCOMBRE AU FROMAGE DE SOYA

Creamy Cucumber Soup with Tofu

Serves: 6
Preparation time: 10 minutes, plus chilling time

The cucumbers grown in the Parisian region, and those from around Bonneuil, have an excellent flavour. For many years it was mandatory to peel cucumbers and remove their seeds, but now it is known that the flavour lies in the skin, not just colour, and the seeds contain the most nourishment.

Imperial (Metric)	American
2 oz (50g) seedless raisins	$\frac{1}{3}$ cup seedless raisins
1 large green cucumber	1 large green cucumber
1 head fennel	1 head fennel
8 oz (225g) silken tofu	1 cup silken tofu
1½ pints (850ml) water	3¾ cups water
Sea salt	Sea salt
Freshly ground black pepper	Freshly ground black pepper
Pinch of ground cumin	Pinch of ground cumin
2 tablespoons snipped chives	2 tablespoons snipped chives
1 sprig dill, finely chopped	1 sprig dill, finely chopped

Soak the raisins in a little boiling water.

Wash the cucumber and slice or dice it.

Separate the fennel into stalks, clean well and slice thinly across.

Place the tofu in a blender with the water and purée to a smooth cream.

Add the fennel to the blender goblet, purée briefly, then add the cucumber and purée again to reduce the mixture to a fine cream. If the mixture is too thick, adjust with a little extra water.

Pour the soup into a serving bowl, season with salt, pepper and cumin, and chill. Serve garnished with chives and dill, adding the soaked and drained raisins at the last minute. A few ice cubes could be floated on the surface of the soup before serving, too.

SOUPE NORMANDE AU CALVADOS

Normandy Vegetable Soup

Serves: 6
Preparation time: 20 minutes
Cooking time: 40 minutes

This thick and warming vegetable soup can be varied to use the best produce available in the market, or the glut in your garden. The traditional Norman ingredient of cream is quite often replaced with tofu by modern vegetarian cooks in France, but it is worth retaining that other item of Normandy produce — Calvados — for a very special soup.

Imperial (Metric)	American
8 oz (225g) runner beans or garden peas	1½ cups green beans or fresh peas
8 oz (225g) sorrel, spinach or lettuce leaves	2 cups sorrel, spinach or lettuce leaves
2 fl oz (50ml) vegetable oil	¼ cup vegetable oil
8 oz (225g) diced potatoes	1⅓ cups diced potato
1 small bunch chives, snipped	1 small bunch chives, snipped
1½ pints (850ml) boiling water	3¾ cups boiling water
2 oz (50g) tofu	¼ cup tofu
Sea salt	Sea salt
Freshly ground black pepper	Freshly ground black pepper
6 slices wholemeal French bread	6 slices whole wheat French bread
2 fl oz (60ml) Calvados	¼ cup Calvados

Top and tail the beans, if using. Cut diagonally into chunks.

Wash whichever leaves you have chosen, removing any coarse stems or damaged pieces. Shred.

Heat the oil in a large pan and sauté the potatoes and chives for 2 minutes, then add the shredded leaves and cook for a further 2 minutes.

Stir in the water, cover, and simmer for 35 minutes or until the potatoes are cooked.

Purée the soup briefly with the tofu. If you have an old-fashioned food mill then use it for this recipe as it will retain the texture that this soup requires.

Reheat the soup and season to taste.

Place a slice of bread in each of six warmed soup bowls, and soak each slice with a little Calvados. Then pour on the soup and serve at once.

Variations: Soya milk could be used instead of tofu, in which case simply stir it in while reheating the soup. Traditionalists may, of course, use cream.

If sorrel is not used, the soup will benefit from the addition of the juice of half a lemon, stirred in when reheating, as this will replace the lost acidity of the sorrel.

POTAGE DE PUY

Rich Lentil Soup

Serves: 6
Preparation time: 15 minutes, plus soaking time
Cooking time: 1 hour 35 minutes

There are many varieties of lentils, all of which can be used to make delicious and nourishing soups. The very best of all are the French lentils de Puy, which are small and green. They take longer to cook than many other varieties, but the flavour is worth the wait!

Imperial (Metric)	American
8 oz (225g) lentils de Puy	1 cup lentils de Puy
1 large onion, chopped	1 large onion, chopped
2 carrots, scrubbed and diced	2 carrots, scrubbed and diced
1 stick celery, chopped	1 stalk celery, chopped
1 stick fennel, chopped	1 stalk fennel, chopped
2 tablespoons peanut oil	2 tablespoons peanut oil
3 cloves garlic, chopped	3 cloves garlic, chopped
1 teaspoon curry powder	1 teaspoon curry powder
1 tablespoon tomato purée	1 tablespoon tomato paste
Sea salt	Sea salt
Freshly ground black pepper	Freshly ground black pepper
Juice of 1 lemon	Juice of 1 lemon

Pick the lentils over thoroughly for stones or other impurities. Wash well, then place in a bowl and cover with cold water. Leave to soak for 3 hours.

Drain the lentils and place in a flameproof casserole with the onion, carrot, celery and fennel.

Cover level with water (about 2½ pints/1½ litres/6 cups), bring to the boil and then simmer for 1½ hours, skimming off any scum as it rises to the surface.

Heat the oil in a small pan and sauté the garlic until tender but not browned. Add the curry powder and cook, stirring, for 30 seconds. Then stir in the tomato purée (paste) and 2 cups of the lentil cooking liquid. Mix well together, then pour this mixture into the pan of lentils.

Pass the soup through a food mill or purée briefly in a blender or food processor — try to achieve a good texture rather than a smooth cream.

Return the soup to the pan to reheat. Season to taste and add the lemon juice just before serving garnished with croûtons or toasted almonds.

SOUPE GLACÉE DE PETITS LÉGUMES AU LAIT DE COCO

Vegetable Soup with Coconut Milk

Preparation time: 15 minutes
Cooking time: 35 minutes, plus chilling time

A real treat, based on a traditional soup of the Nivernais region of France, which was annexed to the Crown under Louis XIV, and where the finest baby turnips are grown.

Imperial (Metric)	American
2 large leeks, white part only	2 large leeks, white part only
12 oz (350g) carrots	4 medium carrots
8 oz (225g) turnips	2 medium turnips
8 oz (225g) new potatoes	4 medium new season potatoes
8 oz (225g) green beans	2 cups green beans
6 oz (150g) desiccated coconut	$\frac{3}{4}$ cup desiccated coconut
1¾ pints (850ml) water	3¾ cups water
1 fl oz (30ml) walnut oil	2 tablespoons walnut oil
Sea salt	Sea salt
Freshly ground black pepper	Freshly ground black pepper
3 sprigs chervil, finely chopped	3 sprigs chervil, finely chopped

Clean the leeks, slice thinly across into rings, wash well and drain.

Scrub the carrots, turnips and potatoes. Dice into small cubes.

Trim the beans and cut into diamonds.

Place the coconut and water in a pan, bring to the boil and simmer for 5 minutes. Pour into a blender and process, then strain to produce a thin, smooth milk.

Heat the oil in a large pan and sauté all the vegetables for 4 minutes. Pour in the coconut milk, bring to the boil and simmer, covered, for 25 minutes.

Cool, season to taste and then chill. Serve garnished with chervil.

Variation: Toasted desiccated coconut might be sprinkled on as an extra garnish.

SOUPE VERDURE DES PRÉS DE SALEUX

Soup of Mixed Green Leaves with Clover

Serves: 6
Preparation time: 15 minutes
Cooking time: 20 minutes, plus chilling time

This is a soup that my grandmother would make every Summer from the produce of her garden. Saleux is a little village west of Amiens, on the Normandy road — the pastures there are green, showing no sign of the battles that scarred the land in the past.

Imperial (Metric)	American
8 oz (225g) sorrel leaves	2 cups sorrel leaves
8 oz (225g) young spinach leaves	2 cups young spinach leaves
1 medium head soft lettuce	1 medium head soft lettuce
6 oz (175g) clover leaves	1½ cups clover leaves
2 small leeks, white part only	2 small leeks, white part only
1 medium onion	1 medium onion
2 tablespoons olive oil	2 tablespoons olive oil
3 sprigs parsley, chopped	3 sprigs parsley, chopped
1½ pints (850ml) boiling water	3¾ cups boiling water
2 oz (50g) toasted almonds	⅓ cup toasted almonds
Sea salt	Sea salt
Freshly ground black pepper	Freshly ground black pepper
2 sprigs chervil or lemon mint, chopped	2 sprigs chervil or lemon mint, chopped

Wash all the leaves well, keeping the clover separate. Remove any tough stems and shred the leaves.

Slice the leeks finely and wash well. Chop the onion.

Heat the oil in a large pan and sauté all the leaves except the clover, along with the leeks, onion and parsley. Cook gently for 5 minutes, stirring all the time.

Pour on the boiling water, stir in half the almonds, cover and simmer for 15 minutes.

Purée the soup in a blender, to form a smooth, pourable liquid.

Allow the soup to cool, then season to taste. Chill and serve, sprinkled with chopped herbs and almonds.

Variations: As an alternative to the almond garnish, toasted croûtons of whole wheat bread could be used.

If sorrel is unavailable, use extra spinach leaves of the same quantity. Rhubarb sticks or green cabbage leaves could also be used. In all these cases, however, the soup should be acidulated with the juice of a lemon.

POTAGE DE TOMATE ET POIVRON AU GINGEMBRE

Rich Tomato and Red Pepper Soup with Ginger

Serves: 6
Preparation time: 15 minutes
Cooking time: 40 minutes, plus chilling time

The large, ribbed tomatoes of the type normally used for stuffing are best for this recipe. This is a hearty soup which is rich in protein due to the addition of the soya curd *tofu*. It is a good introduction to this versatile food for those who have never tried it before.

Imperial (Metric)	American
1 leek, white part only	1 leek, white part only
1½ lb (650g) 'beefsteak' tomatoes	1½ pounds 'beefsteak' tomatoes
1 small piece fresh ginger, peeled and chopped	1 small piece fresh ginger, peeled and chopped
2 cloves garlic, crushed	2 cloves garlic, crushed
1 tablespoon natural soya sauce	1 tablespoon natural soy sauce
6 fl oz (180ml) water	¾ cup water
6 oz (175g) tofu	¾ cup tofu
2 fl oz (60ml) olive oil	¼ cup olive oil
2 large spring onions, chopped	2 large scallions, chopped
1 shallot, chopped	1 shallot, chopped
½ seeded red pepper, chopped	½ seeded red pepper, chopped
1½ pints (850ml) boiling water	3¾ cups boiling water
Sea salt	Sea salt
Freshly ground black pepper	Freshly ground black pepper
4 leaves basil, for garnish	4 leaves basil, for garnish
1 tablespoon chopped chives, for garnish	1 tablespoon chopped chives, for garnish

Thinly slice the leek, wash well, and drain.

Make a nick in the tomato skins, scald briefly in boiling water and remove the skins. Seed and dice neatly into small cubes.

Place the ginger, garlic, soya sauce and water in a blender and purée. Add the tofu and process again very briefly to reduce to a smooth cream.

Heat the oil in a large pan and sauté the spring onions (scallions) and shallot until tender. Add the leek, red pepper and tomato pulp, reserving a little diced tomato for garnish. Sauté for 5 minutes, then add the boiling water. Boil for 15 minutes.

Stir in the tofu mixture and simmer for a further 15 minutes. Chill and season to taste. Serve garnished with the chopped tomato, basil leaves and chives.

Note: Herbs such as chives should be snipped with scissors rather than chopped with a knife, as this retains more of their flavour.

CRÈME AUX FÈVES ALBIGEOISE

Chilled Broad (Fava) Bean Soup with Walnuts

Serves: 6
Preparation time: 15 minutes
Cooking time: 50 minutes, plus chilling time

The nutty flavour of tender young broad (fava) beans marries well with
that of the walnuts in this recipe. I developed this soup when on holiday
with my family in Albi. The walnuts of that region are the best in all
France.

Imperial (Metric)	American
2 lb (900g) broad bean pods	2 pounds fava bean pods
2 medium onions	2 medium onions
1 small shallot	1 small shallot
2 cloves garlic	2 cloves garlic
2 tablespoons walnut oil	2 tablespoons walnut oil
1½ pints (850ml) water	3¾ cups water
2 leaves fresh sage	2 leaves fresh sage
1 small sprig thyme	1 small sprig thyme
1 small sprig winter savory	1 small sprig winter savory
2 oz (50g) chopped walnut kernels	⅓ cup chopped walnut kernels
Sea salt	Sea salt
Freshly ground black pepper	Freshly ground black pepper

Shell the broad (fava) beans and discard the pods.

Peel and chop the onions, shallot and garlic.

Heat the oil in a large pan and sauté the onions and shallots for 3 minutes,
then add the garlic and beans. Cook gently for a further 2 minutes.

Pour the water into the pan, bring to the boil and add the herbs. Cover
and simmer for 45 minutes.

Place the walnuts in a blender with a ladleful of liquid from the soup, and
process until fairly smooth. Stir this mixture into the soup and leave to
cool.

Remove the herbs, chill and serve garnished with fresh chopped sage or
savory, or thin slices of carrot or celery.

POTAGE MIRACLE À LA VANILLE

A 'Three-Pod' Soup with Sesame Seeds

Preparation time: 15 minutes
Cooking time: 50 minutes

This unusual soup was created recently in Lourdes, the miracle town, and is scented with the vanilla pods which are sold in the streets there.

Imperial (Metric)	American
1 lb (450g) runner bean pods	1 pound green beans, in their pods
1 lb (450g) butter beans, in their pods	1 pound Lima beans, in their pods
2 fl oz (60ml) sunflower oil	¼ cup sunflower oil
1 large onion, finely chopped	1 large onion, finely chopped
1 vanilla pod	1 vanilla pod
1½ pints (850ml) boiling water	3¾ cups boiling water
2 oz (50g) toasted sesame seeds	⅓ cup toasted sesame seeds
Sea salt	Sea salt
Freshly ground black pepper	Freshly ground black pepper

Top and tail the bean pods and cut them into thin, diagonal slices.

Heat the oil in a large pan and sauté the onion until soft and translucent. Add the beans and the vanilla pod and sauté gently for a further 5 minutes.

Stir in the boiling water, cover and simmer for 45 minutes.

Pour the soup into a blender or food processor, add the sesame seeds, and process to a creamy emulsion.

Reheat the soup, season to taste, and serve with a garnish of croûtons.

Variations: Non-vegans might like to swirl a little sour cream into the soup before serving.

The vanilla pod can be removed before puréeing if you think the taste will be too strong for your liking, but the flavour is truly exquisite if the vanilla is left in the soup.

BISQUE DE CÉLERI À L'ORANGE

Celery Soup with Ginger and Orange

Serves: 6
Preparation time: 15 minutes
Cooking time: 45 minutes, plus chilling time

In the past soups thickened with crushed hard biscuits were known as *bisques*. In recent times this term has come to be applied to shellfish soups, but here we have a traditional *bisque* in which crumbled ginger biscuits add flavour and texture to a piquant chilled soup.

Imperial (Metric)	American
1 head celery, with leaves	1 head celery, with leaves
3 fl oz (90ml) sunflower oil	$\frac{1}{3}$ cup sunflower oil
1 small onion, chopped	1 small onion, chopped
1 shallot, chopped	1 shallot, chopped
1 medium carrot, cut into thin strips	1 medium carrot, cut into thin strips
$\frac{1}{2}$ teaspoon curry powder	$\frac{1}{2}$ teaspoon curry powder
1$\frac{1}{2}$ pints (850ml) boiling water	3$\frac{3}{4}$ cups boiling water
6 wholemeal ginger biscuits	6 whole wheat ginger biscuits
Sea salt	Sea salt
Freshly ground black pepper	Freshly ground black pepper
Thin strips red pepper, blanched	Thin strips red pepper, blanched
2 seedless oranges, segmented	2 seedless oranges, segmented
Fresh coriander leaves, snipped	Fresh coriander leaves, snipped

Separate the stalks of celery, wash thoroughly and remove any coarse, stringy pieces. Cut into thin slices, across the grain.

Heat the oil in a large saucepan and sauté the onion and shallot until soft but not browned. Add the celery and carrots and sauté for a further 4 minutes. Sprinkle on the curry powder and cook, stirring, for 30 seconds.

Pour on the boiling water, stir well, cover and leave to simmer for 45 minutes.

Place the soup in a blender and process until smooth. Return to the pan and reheat for 5 minutes.

Crush the biscuits with a rolling pin, then stir into the soup. Leave the soup to cool before seasoning with salt and pepper.

Serve chilled, garnished with strips of red pepper and segments of orange, and a sprinkling of chopped fresh coriander.

Variation: Vegans might like to add a swirl of soya milk to this soup for a tasty and nourishing lunch or supper dish.

BOUILLON D'HERBES MARAÎCHÈRES

Fresh Herb Broth

Serves: 6
Preparation time: 15 minutes
Cooking time: 30 minutes

The flavour and aroma of this light soup are appetizing and satisfying, making it perfect for dieters and invalids as well as those who simply appreciate a new and delicious dish to add to their repertoire.

Imperial (Metric)	American
6 lettuce leaves	6 lettuce leaves
6 spinach or chard leaves	6 spinach or chard leaves
$\frac{1}{2}$ bunch watercress	$\frac{1}{2}$ bunch watercress
1 small bunch chives	1 small bunch chives
4 sprigs parsley	4 sprigs parsley
A few leaves tarragon	A few leaves tarragon
1 small sprig thyme	1 small sprig thyme
3 leaves mint	3 leaves mint
2 small leeks	2 small leeks
2 fl oz (60ml) sesame oil	$\frac{1}{4}$ cup sesame oil
2 cloves garlic, crushed	2 cloves garlic, crushed
$1\frac{1}{2}$ pints (850ml) boiling water	$3\frac{3}{4}$ cups boiling water
Sea salt	Sea salt
Freshly ground black pepper	Freshly ground black pepper

Clean and shred all the leaves and herbs, removing any coarse stems.

Trim the leeks, retaining as much of the green part as possible. Slice thinly crosswise and wash well to remove all traces of dirt or grit.

Heat the oil in a large pan and sauté the leeks for 5 minutes. Then add all the leaves, herbs and garlic.

Stir in the water, cover and simmer for 25 minutes. Pass through a food mill or blend briefly.

Reheat, season to taste and serve.

Variations: For a richer soup, 2 oz (50g/$\frac{1}{3}$ cup) walnuts could be puréed with a little of the soup and returned to the pan to reheat and mingle flavours before serving. Alternatively, a little soya milk, sour cream or yogurt could be swirled in when the soup is served.

This soup is also delicious and refreshing served cold, in which case add some ice cubes to each bowl when serving.

LA SOUPE AU CHOU VERT À L'ANANAS

Cabbage Soup with Pineapple

Serves: 6
Preparation time: 20 minutes
Cooking time: 35 minutes

Cabbage soup is traditionally a rustic peasant dish, but the addition of pineapple to the recipe makes this one of the most sophisticated-tasting dishes in this entire chapter.

Imperial (Metric)	American
1 small green cabbage	1 small green cabbage
1 medium onion	1 medium onion
1 large carrot	1 large carrot
1 medium parsnip	1 medium parsnip
2 slices fresh pineapple	2 slices fresh pineapple
2 fl oz (60ml) walnut oil	$\frac{1}{4}$ cup walnut oil
1$\frac{1}{2}$ pints (850ml) boiling water	3$\frac{3}{4}$ cups boiling water
4 oz (100g) walnuts	$\frac{3}{4}$ cup walnuts
1 small piece preserved ginger	1 small piece preserved ginger
1 tablespoon ginger syrup or honey	1 tablespoon ginger syrup or honey
3 fl oz (90ml) soya milk or water	$\frac{1}{3}$ cup soy milk or water
Sea salt	Sea salt
Freshly ground black pepper	Freshly ground black pepper

Separate the cabbage leaves and wash well, removing any coarse stems or damaged pieces. Shred finely.

Peel and chop the onion; scrub and chop the carrot and parsnip. Trim the pineapple.

Heat the oil in a large pan and sauté the onion until translucent. Add the cabbage, carrot and parsnip. Cover and cook for 5 minutes, shaking the pan gently so that all the ingredients cook evenly.

Stir in the boiling water, cover and simmer for 20 minutes.

Place the walnuts, ginger, syrup or honey and milk or water in a blender and purée until smooth. Stir into the soup at the end of its cooking time, and then simmer all together for a further 5 minutes. Season to taste and serve piping hot.

Chapter 2
LES BONNES-BOUCHES

Simple Snacks

A changed pattern of eating is to be found today in homes throughout the Western world, very different to that of the days of my youth. Gone are the big family breakfasts; gone the constant preparation of food by the mother of the house, ready for lunch with children home from school and father back from the fields; gone the dinners and suppers with parents, children, aunts and uncles, grandparents and other relatives gathered around the table all at once. Of course, vestiges remain — perhaps more in France than anywhere, where food and family are so very closely linked. But, for the most part, the modern family is on the move. Relatives are scattered across the country; wives hold down jobs as important as those of their husbands; children dash home from school to run straight out again on missions of intergalactic importance! And where does food fit into this busy life? All too often as an afterthought. As a burger and fries, eaten on the move, or as crisps and an ice-cream in the playground, or as a working lunch, over paperwork in the office, of whatever the snack bar can supply.

But there is a new mood amongst busy and intelligent people, who care about what they and their loved ones eat, and it is in line with this mood that my books are written — this chapter perhaps most of all. Because snacks can be as nutritious as a carefully planned meal. Indeed, it is vital that they should be. They have to supply energy without relying on the short-lived 'high' of sugar or the long-term dangers of fats, and they have to be satisfying to the palate *and* the appetite, so that a tasty treat does not lead to over-indulgence.

The recipes in this chapter have been developed around a loose framework of 4 ounces (100g) of food with a calorific value of about 250 to 300 calories. They are easy to prepare, most can be enjoyed cold as well as hot, and most can be frozen or will keep well for next day's lunch or snack. A salad is all that is needed to turn them into a meal, and a wholemeal roll will provide extra energy for growing youngsters or anyone with a busy physical occupation or recreation. Most revolve around a 'fritter'-type of preparation, using precooked ingredients (leftovers can be transformed into an economical and delicious snack) or quickly prepared fresh ones. This is not an excuse to drench these simple foods in oil — a light coating of the base of a pan, a quick sautéing at the right temperature, and a thorough draining on kitchen paper towels, should add crispness and flavour to your food, not calories.

Protein is not lost at the expense of calories, however. Where dairy produce is not to be found, complete protein is always achieved by the balance of nuts, seeds and pulses. Dishes using dairy foods can be adapted for vegans by the use of soya milk, tofu and soya flour — they will taste just as good, and be just as nutritious.

So try these little morsels in the knowledge that fast food can be good food — both good to eat, and good for you!

CRUCHADES DE SAINTOGNE

Cornmeal Fritters

Serves: 8
Preparation time: 10 minutes, plus cooling time
Cooking time: 8 minutes

The fertile land of the Saintogne region produces much corn, most of which is used these days to feed cattle. But many old recipes survive using corn and cornmeal to good effect in substantial and tasty country dishes.

Imperial (Metric)	American
1¾ pints (1 litre) milk	4½ cups milk
1 level teaspoon sea salt	1 level teaspoon sea salt
2 teaspoons raw cane sugar	2 teaspoons raw cane sugar
8 oz (225g) cornmeal	1¼ cups cornmeal
Freshly ground black pepper	Freshly ground black pepper
Freshly ground mace or nutmeg	Freshly ground mace or nutmeg
1 tablespoon cognac	1 tablespoon cognac
2 tablespoons vegetable oil	2 tablespoons vegetable oil

Bring the milk to the boil and add the salt and sugar. Sprinkle on the cornmeal and stir well. Cook for 6 minutes, stirring to avoid lumps or uneven cooking.

When the mixture is thick, add the other seasonings to taste, and stir in the brandy.

Pour the mixture onto a flat, greased metal tray to cool and set. When set, cut into squares, diamonds or rounds of even size.

Heat the oil in a large frying pan and sauté the corn fritters on each side until golden and sizzling. Serve with a spread, such as the one below.

Variations: **Avocado and Tomato Spread** — peel and mash 1 avocado. Skin, seed and chop 2 large tomatoes and mix with the mashed avocado. Stir in a crushed clove of garlic and a finely chopped spring onion (scallion). Season and use as a spread for the *cruchades*. It can be used as a spread or dip with many other foods, too.

Vegans could substitute a nut milk in this recipe for a tasty snack. Almond milk in particular is very good for this dish.

LES TARTISSEAUX ÉLÉANOR D'AQUITAINE

Cognac and Walnut Buns

Serves: 8
Preparation time: 10 minutes, plus 1½ hours fermenting and resting time
Cooking time: 10 minutes

You will find these little buns — a cross between *brioches* and doughnuts — in the town of La Rochelle, where I spent many years. Most of the town and farm women have their own version of this delightful snack, which can be served at any time of day, with a glass of rosé wine or just a cup of coffee or chocolate.

Imperial (Metric)	American
1 lb (450g) wholemeal flour	4 cups whole wheat flour
1 level teaspoon sea salt	1 level teaspoon sea salt
3 free-range eggs	3 free-range eggs
¾ oz (20g) fresh yeast	Scant 2 tablespoons fresh yeast
3 fl oz (90ml) warm water	⅓ cup warm water
2 fl oz (60ml) vegetable oil, or butter	¼ cup vegetable oil, or melted butter
2 tablespoons cognac	2 tablespoons cognac
2 oz (50g) chopped walnuts	½ cup chopped walnuts
Vegetable oil for frying	Vegetable oil for frying

Sift the flour into a large bowl with the sea salt, tipping back any bran left in the sieve.

Beat the eggs, make a well in the flour and gently stir in the eggs until well mixed.

Cream the yeast with the warm water until smooth. Blend this mixture into the flour and eggs, ensuring that everything is completely mixed. Leave to ferment for 10 minutes.

After 10 minutes, knead the mixture to a smooth dough. Roll into a ball, cover with a damp cloth and leave to prove for 20 minutes.

Punch down the dough, adding the oil or butter until blended into the dough. Cover the dough again and leave to rest for 15 minutes.

Punch the dough down again and knead in the brandy and nuts. Cover and leave to rise to twice its volume. The resulting dough should be of a soft, dropping consistency.

Form the dough into balls the size of an egg. Roll them in a light dusting of flour and leave to rest for 12 minutes.

Heat vegetable oil in a large pan — for safety, the oil should not come to more than half-way up the sides of the pan.

Fry the buns a few at a time for 3 minutes, turning in the oil to ensure even cooking. Drain on kitchen paper towels and serve warm, with a compote of fruit.

LES MOGETTES À LA CHARENTAISE

Mushrooms Stuffed with a Rich Bean Purée

Preparation time: 10 minutes, plus cooling time
Cooking time: 55 minutes

The fresh young haricot (navy) beans of Courçon-d'Aunis were the inspiration for this variation on a traditional dish of the region. Their nutty flavour is enhanced by the other stuffing ingredients, making a simple dish of stuffed mushrooms into a gourmet treat.

Imperial (Metric)	American
2 fl oz (60ml) olive oil	$\frac{1}{4}$ cup olive oil
1 shallot, chopped	1 shallot, chopped
2 cloves garlic, crushed	2 cloves garlic, crushed
8 oz (225g) fresh, shelled haricot beans	1$\frac{1}{3}$ cups fresh, shelled navy beans
2 fl oz (60ml) red Bordeaux wine	$\frac{1}{4}$ cup red Bordeaux wine
$\frac{1}{2}$ pint (300ml) water, approx.	1$\frac{1}{3}$ cups water, approx.
1 oz (25g) tomato purée	2 tablespoons tomato paste
Sea salt	Sea salt
Freshly ground black pepper	Freshly ground black pepper
2 oz (50g) chopped pine nuts	$\frac{1}{4}$ cup chopped pignoli
8 large, cupped mushrooms	8 large, cupped mushrooms
8 slices toasted French bread	8 slices toasted French bread

Heat the oil in a large pan and sauté the shallot and garlic for 1 minute only.

Add the beans to the pan, then stir in the wine and enough water to just cover the beans. Cover the pan and simmer very gently for 45 minutes.

Stir in the tomato purée (paste), season lightly, and then mash the bean mixture to a coarse purée. Stir the chopped nuts into this mixture and set aside to cool. Check seasoning when cold.

Clean the mushrooms carefully. Remove the stems, chop them finely and add them to the bean paste.

Fill the mushroom caps with the bean stuffing, spreading it neatly to fill each cap completely. Brush with a very little oil, place on an oiled baking tray and cook in a hot oven (450°F/230°C/Gas Mark 8) for 8 minutes. Serve at once on the toasted bread.

LES CROQUES-SEIGNEURS

Spicy Sautéd Peanut Sandwiches

Serves: 2 as a light meal; 4 as a snack
Preparation time: 5 minutes
Cooking time: 4 minutes

Here is an exotic variation on the classic French snack of *Croque-Monsieur*, which I guarantee everyone — especially children — will adore.

Imperial (Metric)	American
1½ oz (45g) roasted peanuts	3 tablespoons roasted peanuts
2 free-range egg yolks	2 free-range egg yolks
4 large slices wholemeal bread	4 large slices whole wheat bread
2 large free-range eggs	2 large free-range eggs
2 fl oz (60ml) buttermilk	¼ cup buttermilk
Sea salt	Sea salt
Freshly ground black pepper	Freshly ground black pepper
1 teaspoon curry powder	1 teaspoon curry powder
1 clove garlic, crushed	1 clove garlic, crushed
1 tablespoon finely chopped fresh parsley	1 tablespoon finely chopped fresh parsley
1 tablespoon toasted sesame seeds	1 tablespoon toasted sesame seeds
Peanut oil, for frying	Peanut oil, for frying

In a blender, purée together the peanuts and egg yolks.

Cut each slice of bread in half, and spread the peanut paste onto one half of each slice. Sandwich firmly together.

In a large, shallow bowl (a soup plate would do perfectly) beat together the eggs, buttermilk, salt, pepper, curry powder, garlic, parsley and sesame seeds.

Heat a little oil in a pan. Lay two sandwiches in the egg mixture, first on one side, then the other, so that they are well coated. Then place them in the hot oil and cook until golden brown on both sides — about 2 minutes. Drain well.

Keep warm while the remaining sandwiches are cooked. Serve with a salad of beansprouts and grapefruit segments for a delicious and satisfying light meal, or eat the *croques* hot from the pan as a savoury snack.

LES DORINES AUX MARRONS

Chestnut Tartlets

Serves: 8
Preparation time: 45 minutes
Cooking time: 25 to 30 minutes

This delicate tartlet belongs to the Auvergne region, where chestnuts abound. It is usually served as a dessert, flavoured with plenty of sugar, but I have chosen to omit this in favour of a savoury dish, which I feel brings out the mellow taste of the chestnuts to pleasing effect.

Imperial (Metric)	American
For the pastry:	*For the pastry:*
3 oz (75g) vegetable margarine	⅓ cup vegetable margarine
1 free-range egg yolk	1 free-range egg yolk
6 oz (150g) wholemeal flour	1½ cups whole wheat flour
Sea salt	Sea salt
1 tablespoon water	1 tablespoon water
For the custard:	*For the custard:*
½ pint (300ml) milk	1⅓ cups milk
3 free-range egg yolks	3 free-range egg yolks
1 tablespoon cornmeal	1 tablespoon cornmeal
Sea salt	Sea salt
Freshly grated nutmeg	Freshly grated nutmeg
For the filling:	*For the filling:*
6 oz (150g) chestnut purée	1 cup chestnut paste
1 oz (25g) curd cheese	2 tablespoons curd cheese
1 crushed clove garlic, or	1 crushed clove garlic, or
1 tablespoon snipped chives	1 tablespoon snipped chives
Pinch freshly grated nutmeg	Pinch freshly grated nutmeg

Prepare the pastry by creaming together in a bowl the margarine and egg. Gradually add the flour and salt to form a stiff dough, then stir in the water to achieve the correct consistency for pastry. Cover the dough and refrigerate for 30 minutes.

Meanwhile, prepare the custard. Bring the milk to a boil. Beat the egg yolks with the cornmeal, salt and nutmeg in a bowl and gradually add the hot milk, stirring constantly to achieve a smooth paste. Return the mixture to the pan and reheat gently for 2 minutes to thicken the custard. Cool.

Beat together the chestnut purée (paste), cheese, garlic or chives and nutmeg.

Divide the dough into eight equal pieces. Roll out each to line greased individual tartlet moulds.

Half fill the pastry bases with chestnut mixture. Top each with the cooled savoury custard.

Bake the tartlets in a preheated oven at 400°F/200°C (Gas Mark 6) for 20 to 25 minutes, until risen and golden. Serve hot or cold.

PETITS CLAFOUTIS AUX LÉGUMES

Little Vegetable Tartlets

Makes: 10 tartlets
Preparation time: 15 minutes
Cooking time: 25 to 30 minutes

This is a recipe from Picardy — in particular from the region of Crécy, still best known for the spectacular victory of King Edward III of England over King Philippe de Valois of France in 1346.

Imperial (Metric)	*American*
For the batter:	*For the batter:*
2 oz (50g) vegetable margarine	$\frac{1}{4}$ cup vegetable margarine
5 oz (125g) wholemeal flour	$1\frac{1}{4}$ cups whole wheat flour
1 teaspoon baking powder	1 teaspoon baking powder
1 oz (25g) soya flour	$\frac{1}{4}$ cup soy flour
1 oz (25g) ground almonds	$\frac{1}{4}$ cup ground almonds
$\frac{1}{4}$ teaspoon sea salt	$\frac{1}{4}$ teaspoon sea salt
3 free-range eggs, beaten	3 free-range eggs, beaten
$\frac{1}{4}$ pint (150ml) water	$\frac{2}{3}$ cup water
Sea salt	Sea salt
Freshly ground black pepper	Freshly ground black pepper
For the filling:	*For the filling:*
2 oz (50 g) cooked peas	$\frac{1}{3}$ cup cooked peas
2 oz (50g) diced cooked carrots	$\frac{1}{3}$ cup diced cooked carrots
2 oz (50g) blanched cauliflower florets	$\frac{1}{2}$ cup blanched cauliflower florets
2 oz (50g) chopped shallots	$\frac{1}{3}$ cup chopped shallots
2 oz (50g) blanched broccoli florets	$\frac{1}{2}$ cup blanched broccoli florets
2 oz (50g) blanched sweetcorn	$\frac{1}{3}$ cup blanched corn kernels
2 oz (50g) cooked red kidney beans	$\frac{1}{3}$ cup cooked red kidney beans
1 oz (25g) chopped red pepper	2 tablespoons chopped red pepper

Grease 10 foil or metal tartlet moulds (100ml capacity) with the margarine.

Stir all the dry batter ingredients together in a large bowl. In another bowl beat together the eggs and water. Gradually add this to the dry ingredients, beating well to form a thick batter. Check seasoning, then set the batter aside to rest.

In a bowl, mix together all the vegetables. Divide this mixture equally between the 10 moulds, then top up each mould with batter.

Place the moulds on a baking tray and bake on the high shelf of the oven at 400°F/200°C (Gas Mark 6) for 25 to 30 minutes. Serve hot or cold.

LES FAYOTS À LA NAPOLÉON

Bean 'Burger' Salad Sandwiches

Makes: 8 sandwiches
Preparation time: 5 minutes
Cooking time: 10 minutes

This is a dish the essence of which stems from the days when Napoleon's army was sweeping across Europe. In those days, a soldier's diet was very much reliant on beans, known then as *fayot*. Nowadays the word has become slang for any common, humble dish. Not so these piquant morsels, whose rich flavours reflect the influence of the many Spaniards who fought in *la Grande Armée*.

Imperial (Metric)	American
Olive oil, for frying	Olive oil, for frying
1 onion, chopped	1 onion, chopped
3 cloves garlic, chopped	3 cloves garlic, chopped
2 oz (50g) toasted sesame seeds	$\frac{1}{4}$ cup toasted sesame seeds
3 oz (75g) roasted peanuts	$\frac{1}{2}$ cup roasted peanuts
8 oz (225g) cooked beans of choice	1½ cups cooked beans of choice
1 oz (25g) tomato purée	2 tablespoons tomato paste
Sea salt	Sea salt
Freshly ground black pepper	Freshly ground black pepper
1 oz (25g) wholemeal flour	$\frac{1}{4}$ cup whole wheat flour
For the filling:	*For the filling:*
1 ripe avocado, peeled and sliced	1 ripe avocado, peeled and sliced
2 large tomatoes, sliced	2 large tomatoes, sliced
1 large onion, thinly sliced	1 large onion, thinly sliced
1 green chilli, thinly sliced	1 green chili, thinly sliced
Lettuce leaves	Lettuce leaves

Heat a little oil in a large pan and sauté the onion for 2 minutes. Stir in the garlic, seeds and nuts and cook for another minute.

Add the beans and tomato purée (paste), and cook for 4 more minutes, stirring frequently.

Cool the mixture slightly, then mash to a coarse paste. Season to taste.

Divide the mixture into 16 small cakes. Dust each side with flour, shaking off any excess.

Heat some oil in a large frying pan and sauté batches of bean cakes until golden and sizzling on both sides. This should only take about a minute for each batch. Keep cooked bean cakes warm on kitchen paper towels until ready to serve.

Place a little of each of the filling ingredients on 8 of the 'burgers', and top each with one of the remaining batch. Serve hot or cold on crisp lettuce leaves.

Note: Remove the seeds from the chilli if you find them too hot — or leave this ingredient out altogether, replacing it with a light sprinkling of paprika.

LES PETITS POIS DE CHANIERS EN GALETTE

Green Pea Fritters with Buttermilk

Preparation time: 10 minutes, plus cooling time
Cooking time: 6 minutes

The Charente is known for its deliciously tender peas, and the many local recipes for cooking them are just as appetizing. This dish is often served as a garnish, but is so good that it makes a tasty snack on its own, and is a good way of using up cooked peas, too.

Imperial (Metric)	American
8 oz (225g) tiny garden peas	1⅓ cups tiny fresh peas
2 oz (50g) diced carrots	⅓ cup diced carrots
2 oz (50g) chopped walnuts	⅓ cup chopped walnuts
2 fl oz (60ml) buttermilk	¼ cup buttermilk
1 free-range egg, beaten	1 free-range egg, beaten
1 oz (25g) wholemeal breadcrumbs	½ cup whole wheat breadcrumbs
Sea salt	Sea salt
Freshly ground black pepper	Freshly ground black pepper
2 fl oz (60ml) vegetable oil	¼ cup vegetable oil

Cook the peas and carrots together for 6 minutes, then drain and refresh under cold water. Drain well.

Mince the vegetables and nuts together in a blender or food processor, without puréeing too finely.

Place the mixture in a bowl and beat in the buttermilk, egg and breadcrumbs. Season lightly, and allow to cool.

When the mixture is cold, shape into 8 small balls and then flatten these into little cakes.

Heat the oil in a pan and cook the fritters in batches, frying quickly on both sides until golden-brown. Serve piping hot, or cold.

CROQUEMITAINES AU RUTABAGA

Potato and Swede (Rutabaga) Croquettes

Preparation time: 10 minutes
Cooking time: 25 minutes

There was a time in France when swedes (rutabaga) were only used as cattle-feed, but the new approach to cookery has begun to rediscover the tasty, traditional recipes using this delicious vegetable. Here is just such a dish, from Boulogne where I was raised.

Imperial (Metric)	American
8 oz (225g) swedes	8 ounces rutabaga
8 oz (225g) potatoes	8 ounces potatoes
3 free-range eggs, beaten	3 free-range eggs, beaten
1 oz (25g) soya flour	$\frac{1}{4}$ cup soy flour
1 oz (25g) ground almonds	$\frac{1}{4}$ cup ground almonds
1 oz (25g) curd cheese	$\frac{1}{4}$ cup curd cheese
Sea salt	Sea salt
Freshly ground black pepper	Freshly ground black pepper
1 oz (25g) wholemeal flour	$\frac{1}{4}$ cup whole wheat flour
2 oz (50g) flaked almonds	$\frac{1}{2}$ cup slivered almonds
2 fl oz (60ml) vegetable oil	$\frac{1}{4}$ cup vegetable oil

Wash the vegetables, peel if necessary, and slice. Boil in plenty of salted water for 15 minutes, or until tender. Drain well, then return the vegetables to the pan and warm over a very low heat to drive off any remaining water.

Pass the vegetables through a food mill, and leave to cool.

When cold, beat in two-thirds of the eggs, along with the soya flour, almonds and cheese. Season to taste.

Divide the mixture into 16 small balls. Flatten into croquettes.

Spread the flour out on one plate, pour the remaining beaten egg onto another, and spread the almonds onto a third. Pass each croquette through each of these in order.

Heat the oil in a shallow pan and sauté the croquettes in batches until golden-brown on both sides. Drain well on absorbent paper and serve hot.

LES CROQUIGNOLES DE POMMES AUX GRAINES

Seeded Potato and Corn Cakes

Makes: 16 cakes
Preparation time: 5 minutes
Cooking time: 8 minutes

When the potato arrived in France from the New World it was grown as an ornamental plant, and it was not until 1770 that Antoine Parmentier, the then Minister of Agriculture, instigated its cultivation as a vegetable to help overcome food shortages. The debt of honour we owe that inventive man is acknowledged in the many potato dishes and garnishes that bear his name.

Imperial (Metric)	American
8 oz (225g) peeled, washed and grated potato	2 cups peeled, washed and grated potato
1 small onion, finely chopped	1 small onion, finely chopped
1 clove garlic, crushed	1 clove garlic, crushed
3 oz (75g) blanched sweetcorn	½ cup blanched corn kernels
1 tablespoon chopped fresh parsley	1 tablespoon chopped fresh parsley
2 large free-range eggs, beaten	2 large free-range eggs, beaten
1½ tablespoons wholemeal flour	1½ tablespoons whole wheat flour
1 tablespoon toasted sesame seeds	1 tablespoon toasted sesame seeds
1 tablespoon toasted sunflower seeds	1 tablespoon toasted sunflower seeds
1 tablespoon toasted flaked almonds	1 tablespoon toasted flaked almonds
1 teaspoon cumin seeds	1 teaspoon cumin seeds
Sea salt	Sea salt
Freshly ground black pepper	Freshly ground black pepper
Vegetable oil, for frying	Vegetable oil, for frying

In a large bowl, beat together all the ingredients except the oil, to form a stiff batter.

Heat a little oil in a large frying pan and drop in heaped tablespoons of the mixture, 4 at a time, to sauté. They will spread to form little pancakes. When golden underneath, turn and sauté until cooked on the other side.

Serve hot or cold. They are delicious spread with cream cheese, mashed avocado, bean purée or other topping, and sprinkled with extra toasted sesame seeds.

LA CAILLEBOTTE À LA CHARDONNETTE

Curd Cheese with Cognac

Preparation time: 20 minutes
Cooking time: 3 minutes

This dish comes from the rich province of Poitou-Charentes, which also produces France's finest brandy — Cognac. Naturally, it features in many of the recipes of that region, including this one.

Imperial (Metric)	American
$\frac{1}{3}$–$\frac{1}{2}$ oz (8–10g) dried artichoke flowers (*chardonnette*)	$\frac{1}{3}$ to $\frac{1}{2}$ cup dried artichoke flowers (*chardonnette*)
1$\frac{3}{4}$ pints (1 litre) milk or single cream	4$\frac{1}{2}$ cups milk or light cream
Sea salt	Sea salt
Freshly ground black pepper	Freshly ground black pepper
2 fl oz (60ml) cognac	$\frac{1}{4}$ cup cognac

Wrap the artichoke flowers tightly in muslin and tie firmly.

Place the milk or cream in a pan and heat until tepid (110°F/60°C). Remove the pan from the heat and immerse the artichoke flowers in the milk, pressing the muslin bag with the back of a wooden spoon to extract the juices. Cover and leave for 10 minutes, or until the milk has curdled.

Line a colander with clean muslin and pour the curds and whey into this and drain. Press to extract all the moisture.

When the curds are firm, season to taste and then shape into small balls. Sprinkle with cognac and serve with crackers or dry toast.

Variations: Caillebotte can be flavoured with snipped chives, fresh herbs or crushed garlic, or rolled in chopped nuts. Shaped into larger balls it can be deep fried briefly and served with a sharp conserve for an elegant appetizer.

CASSE-CROÛTE AUX PETITS POIS À LA MARSEILLAISE

Spicy French Bread Sandwich

Preparation time: 5 minutes, plus cooling time
Cooking time: 20 minutes

Try to find an authentic *baguette* or French stick for this tasty sandwich. Eat it as soon as it is made for a satisfying, crunchy snack, or wrap in foil for later as a more mellow — but just as satisfying — picnic or lunchbox treat.

Imperial (Metric)	American
2 fl oz (60ml) walnut oil	¼ cup walnut oil
1 small onion, chopped	1 small onion, chopped
2 cloves garlic, crushed	3 cloves garlic, crushed
8 oz (225g) fresh shelled peas	1¼ cups fresh shelled peas
1 large tomato, skinned, seeded and chopped	1 large tomato, skinned, seeded and chopped
2 oz (50g) chopped walnuts	¼ cup chopped walnuts
Sea salt	Sea salt
Freshly ground black pepper	Freshly ground black pepper
1 large French stick	1 large French stick
4 crisp lettuce leaves	4 crisp lettuce leaves

Heat the oil in a pan and sauté the onion for 2 minutes, until it begins to soften. Add the garlic and cook briefly.

Add the peas, stir, then pour in just enough water to cover. Bring to the boil and then simmer for about 15 minutes, skimming off any scum that rises. When the peas are tender, stir in the tomatoes and walnuts.

Cook the mixture briefly, then strain. The liquid can be used as a stock for soup. Season the pea mixture to taste.

Mince or mash the pea mixture. Leave to cool.

Cut the bread into four lengths and split in half. Lay a lettuce leaf on each piece — there is no need to butter the bread. Top the lettuce leaf with a generous portion of the pea mixture and sandwich the bread back together. Serve with a glass of country wine or cider for a real treat.

TARTELETTE AU FROMAGE DE SOYA

Tofu Tartlet

Makes: 8 tartlets
Preparation time: 15 minutes
Cooking time: 25 minutes

Soya bean curd or tofu replaces the traditional cream cheese in this nourishing snack. It is a protein-rich substance whose bland taste absorbs the flavours put with it, so do not be afraid to season your tartlets well.

Imperial (Metric)	American
For the pastry:	*For the pastry:*
8 oz (225g) wholemeal flour	2 cups whole wheat flour
1 teaspoon baking powder	1 teaspoon baking powder
Sea salt	Sea salt
3 oz (75g) polyunsaturated margarine	$\frac{1}{3}$ cup polyunsaturated margarine
2 oz (50g) dry mashed potato	$\frac{1}{4}$ cup dry mashed potato
For the filling:	*For the filling:*
8 oz (225g) silken tofu	1 cup silken tofu
2 free-range eggs, beaten	2 free-range eggs, beaten
1 small shallot, finely chopped	1 small shallot, finely chopped
Sea salt	Sea salt
Freshly ground black pepper	Freshly ground black pepper
1 oz (25g) flaked almonds	$\frac{1}{4}$ cup slivered almonds

Place the flour in a bowl and stir in the baking powder and some salt. Rub in the margarine, then beat in the mashed potato. Add a little warm water to make a smooth dough and knead gently into a ball.

Divide the dough into 8 pieces and flatten them evenly into 8 small, greased tartlet tins. Prick the bottom of each tartlet.

Beat the tofu with the eggs until fluffy, then stir in the chopped shallot. Season well. Sprinkle almonds over the top of each tartlet.

Bake in a preheated oven at 400°F/200°C (Gas Mark 6) for about 20 minutes, on the middle shelf, until golden and risen. Serve hot or cold.

Note: The shallot could be replaced with 2 oz (50g/$\frac{1}{4}$ cup) seedless raisins.

Chapter 3
LES SALADES TIÈDES

Salads of Contrast

To my mind, one of the most interesting ideas to come out of the *nouvelle cuisine* is the concept of marrying hot and cold ingredients in a salad. The idea began with the addition of freshly fried croûtons, or *lardons* of bacon being tipped, still sizzling, onto salad leaves. But, of course, it has always been recognized that ingredients such as potatoes or pulses absorb a dressing much better while still warm, and this fact has been incorporated into the style by serving them while still warm.

So many wonderful salad ingredients are now readily available in our shops that the vegetarian has no need to add meat or poultry to a salad in order to make an appetizing dish. No longer is just one lettuce to be found — a wealth of colours and shapes are on display as salad leaves, each one with its own personality to add to your dish. For a more substantial dish, pasta, grains, pulses and seeds give body and protein, even to the point where a salad can become a meal in itself. Eggs and cheese provide a vegetarian diner with yet more protein, and recently tofu has become more widely available to provide the vegan diner with a nourishing salad meal.

If the day is hot, and a salad takes your fancy, you will find that most of the recipes in this section can be served cold as well as warm, with no loss of flavour or character. But do try this interesting balance of hot and cold. It is one that gourmets love, and really it is no more unusual than that classic children's favourite of ice-cream with a hot chocolate or caramel sauce! Hot and cold, contrasted together, bring out unexpected depths of flavour in even a simple dish. Sample the dishes in this chapter and I feel sure you will not be disappointed.

LA FRISÉE DE PICARDIE AUX POIS CHICHES

Chick Pea and Endive (Chicory) Salad

Preparation time: 10 minutes
Cooking time: 20 minutes

Endive (chicory) has a distinctive, bitter flavour which is pleasantly offset by the creamy, nutty taste of the chick peas in this appetizing and protein-rich salad.

Imperial (Metric)	American
For the dressing:	*For the dressing:*
1 teaspoon Dijon mustard	1 teaspoon Dijon mustard
1 oz (25g) chopped walnuts	$\frac{1}{4}$ cup chopped walnuts
1 clove garlic, chopped	1 clove garlic, chopped
4 oz (100g) silken tofu	$\frac{1}{2}$ cup silken tofu
1 small shallot, finely chopped	1 small shallot, finely chopped
3 fl oz (90ml) apple juice	$\frac{1}{3}$ cup apple juice
1 tablespoon cider vinegar	1 tablespoon cider vinegar
Sea salt	Sea salt
Freshly ground black pepper	Freshly ground black pepper
For the salad:	*For the salad:*
8 oz (225g) new potatoes	8 ounces new season potatoes
1 medium head endive	1 medium head chicory
1 medium tin chick peas	1 medium can chick peas
4 quail's eggs (optional)	4 quail's eggs (optional)
2 red-skinned apples	2 red-skinned apples
2 oz (50g) chopped walnuts	$\frac{1}{2}$ cup chopped walnuts
1 tablespoon snipped chives	1 tablespoon snipped chives

Place all the dressing ingredients in a blender and blend until smooth. Set aside for the flavours to mingle and develop.

Boil the new potatoes for 20 minutes in plenty of salted water until tender.

Meanwhile, separate the salad leaves and wash well, discarding any damaged leaves. Drain well.

Heat the chick peas gently in their liquid.

Boil the quail's eggs for 6 minutes.

Arrange the salad leaves on individual plates or a large platter. Core the apples neatly and cut into thin triangles. Arrange on the endive (chicory).

Drain the potatoes, chick peas and quail's eggs. Slice the potatoes and arrange attractively on the plate, perhaps as a border to the leaves, or as a central flower-shape. Scatter chick peas and walnuts over the salad, and place a quail's egg on each portion.

Drizzle a little dressing over all the ingredients, scatter with chives, and serve at once, so that the eggs, chick peas and potatoes are still warm.

LA SALADE FLAMANDE DE PETITS POIS AUX NOIX D'ACAJOU

Flemish Green Pea and Nut Salad

Serves: 8 as a side salad; 6 as a main course
Preparation time: 10 minutes
Cooking time: 12 minutes

Peas, corn and cashew nuts give an excellent protein balance in this hearty country salad, and the addition of tofu to the dressing really makes it a meal in itself.

Imperial (Metric)	American
For the dressing:	*For the dressing:*
5 oz (150g) silken tofu	Generous $\frac{1}{2}$ cup silken tofu
4 mint leaves	4 mint leaves
2 tablespoons sherry vinegar	2 tablespoons sherry vinegar
Juice of 1 lemon	Juice of 1 lemon
Juice of 1 orange	Juice of 1 orange
2 teaspoons natural soya sauce	2 teaspoons natural soy sauce
For the salad:	*For the salad:*
2 lb (900g) fresh peas	2 pounds fresh peas
8 oz (225g) diced carrot	$1\frac{1}{3}$ cups diced carrot
8 oz (225g) sweetcorn	$1\frac{1}{3}$ cups fresh corn kernels
Sea salt	Sea salt
Freshly ground black pepper	Freshly ground black pepper
1 small radicchio	1 small radicchio
1 small round lettuce heart	1 small round lettuce heart
5 oz (150g) cashew nuts	$\frac{3}{4}$ cup cashew nuts

Place all the ingredients for the dressing in a blender and blend to a smooth cream. Set aside for the flavours to mingle and develop. The mixture will be quite thick.

Shuck the peas and discard the pods. Bring a large pan of salted water to the boil and cook the peas, carrots and corn for 12 minutes. Drain, reserving 2 tablespoons of the cooking liquid. Refresh the vegetables briefly under cold running water, then drain again.

Stir the cooking liquid into the dressing to thin slightly. Place the vegetables in a large bowl, and pour half the dressing over them. Season and toss everything well to coat in the dressing.

Separate the salad leaves. Wash well and drain. Arrange on individual plates.

Spoon some of the vegetable mixture onto each plate and sprinkle with cashew nuts. Serve at once, offering the rest of the dressing separately.

LA SALADE DE CHOU-FLEUR AU SAFRAN

Cauliflower Salad with Saffron

Preparation time: 10 minutes
Cooking time: 11 minutes

The saffron in this recipe tints the cauliflower a beautiful golden-yellow.
Combined with the pale green lettuce leaves and the optional yellow and
white of chopped hard-boiled eggs, its spring-like appearance will brighten
even the dullest of days.

Imperial (Metric)	American
1 medium cauliflower	1 medium cauliflower
2 fl oz (60ml) olive oil	$\frac{1}{4}$ cup olive oil
1 small onion, chopped	1 small onion, chopped
2 cloves garlic, crushed	2 cloves garlic, crushed
2 fl oz (60ml) dry white wine	$\frac{1}{4}$ cup dry white wine
1 small sachet powdered saffron	1 small sachet powdered saffron
4 fl oz (120ml) natural yogurt	$\frac{1}{2}$ cup plain yogurt
2 oz (50g) seedless raisins	$\frac{1}{3}$ cup seedless raisins
1 green chilli, seeded and sliced	1 green chili, seeded and sliced
Sea salt	Sea salt
Freshly ground black pepper	Freshly ground black pepper
1 round lettuce heart	1 round lettuce heart
4 diced hard-boiled free-range eggs (optional)	4 diced hard-cooked free-range eggs (optional)
Juice of 1 lemon	Juice of 1 lemon

Separate the cauliflower into small florets. Wash and drain well.

Heat the oil in a large frying pan and sauté the onion and garlic for 30
seconds only. Then stir in the cauliflower and stir-fry, without browning,
for a minute.

Add the wine and saffron, cover the pan and cook gently for 10 minutes.

Remove the pan from the heat and beat in the yogurt, raisins, chilli and
seasoning.

Separate the lettuce leaves. Rinse and drain well, and arrange on
individual serving plates. Spoon the cauliflower mixture over this.

Sprinkle the salad with egg, if used, and squeeze lemon juice over each plate just before serving.

Variations: Vegans could substitute silken tofu for the yogurt. Fresh seedless grapes could be used instead of raisins, or the raisins could be soaked in hot liquid to help them swell, before being drained and added to the salad.

LA SALADE NOISETIÈRE

Hazelnut Salad

Preparation time: 10 minutes
Cooking time: 3 minutes

My grandmother Mathilde used to make this salad, and would send the children out to gather hazelnuts from the local woods, dandelion leaves from the meadows around the house, and large white Bigarreaux cherries from the tree in the garden.

Imperial (Metric)	American
For the dressing:	*For the dressing:*
1 oz (25g) toasted hazelnuts	¼ cup toasted hazelnuts
3 fl oz (90ml) buttermilk	⅓ cup buttermilk
2 fl oz (60ml) sherry vinegar	¼ cup sherry vinegar
1 teaspoon Dijon mustard	1 teaspoon Dijon mustard
1 teaspoon clear honey	1 teaspoon clear honey
Sea salt	Sea salt
Freshly ground black pepper	Freshly ground black pepper
For the salad:	*For the salad:*
1 round letttuce heart	1 round lettuce heart
6 spring onions	6 scallions
1 small white radish (mooli)	1 small white radish (mooli)
8 oz (225g) white cherries	2 cups white cherries
8 oz (225g) shelled hazelnuts	1½ cups hazelnut kernels

Place all the dressing ingredients in a blender and blend to a smooth cream. Set aside for the flavours to develop and mingle.

Separate the lettuce leaves. Wash and drain well, then arrange on four individual serving plates.

Thinly slice the spring onions (scallions) diagonally. Peel the radish and cut into thin slices. Scatter both vegetables over the lettuce, or arrange in an attractive mound in the centre of each plate.

Stone (pit) the cherries and decorate the plates with them.

Toast the hazelnuts in a dry, heavy-based pan for 3 minutes, until evenly browned. Scatter these over each plate and serve at once, offering dressing in a sauce boat for your guests or family to serve themselves.

PANACHÉ DE FEUILLES DE CHÊNE AUX HARICOTS VERTS

Oak Leaf and Bean Salad

Preparation time: 10 minutes
Cooking time: 7 minutes

Oak leaf lettuce is similar in flavour to endive and chicory. Its attractive shape and colour lends style even to the simplest of salads. Here it is teamed with the succulent 'bite' of tender French beans and golden kernels of corn for a charming and delicious presentation.

Imperial (Metric)	American
1 oak leaf lettuce	1 oak leaf lettuce
8 oz (225g) French beans	1½ cups string beans
2 fl oz (60ml) olive oil	¼ cup olive oil
2 shallots, chopped	2 shallots, chopped
4 cloves garlic, crushed	4 cloves garlic, crushed
Sea salt	Sea salt
Freshly ground black pepper	Freshly ground black pepper
2 oz (50g) sweetcorn	⅓ cup corn kernels
2 oz (50g) chopped walnuts	½ cup chopped walnuts
2 tablespoons sherry vinegar	2 tablespoons sherry vinegar
2 oz (50g) seedless muscat grapes	½ cup seedless muscat grapes

Separate the lettuce into leaves, discarding any damaged ones. Wash and drain well. Arrange the leaves on individual serving plates.

Blanch the beans for 5 minutes in boiling salted water, then plunge into ice cold water to retain the colour, and drain well.

Heat the oil in a pan and sauté the shallots and garlic briefly, then add the beans and stir-fry for 2 minutes. Season lightly, then spoon out onto the lettuce leaves.

Sprinkle the corn and walnuts onto the salads, then drizzle with a little sherry vinegar, to balance out the olive oil. Decorate the plates with grapes and serve at once.

LA SALADE DE CANTALOUP AUX CHAMPIGNONS

Melon and Mushroom Salad

Preparation time: 10 minutes, plus 15 minutes marinating time

This refreshing salad of two melons with mushrooms and lettuce, in a dressing of white port, is as lovely to eat as it is to look at.

Imperial (Metric)	American
1lb (450g) button mushrooms	1 pound button mushrooms
5 spring onions	5 scallions
1 cos lettuce	1 romaine lettuce
½ small watermelon	½ small watermelon
1 small yellow-fleshed melon	1 small yellow-fleshed melon
2 fl oz (60ml) white port	¼ cup white port
2 tablespoons olive oil	2 tablespoons olive oil
1 small piece preserved ginger	1 small piece preserved ginger
Sea salt	Sea salt
Freshly ground black pepper	Freshly ground black pepper

Clean the mushrooms well, trimming the stems off (these can be used for another dish).

Thinly slice the spring onions (scallions) diagonally, using as much of the green part as possible.

Separate the lettuce leaves. Wash and drain well, and arrange on four individual serving plates. Scatter with the onion slices.

Slice the watermelon in half lengthways. Trim the skin from one half and cut into thin slices. Arrange these decoratively on the serving plates — it is worth retaining the seeds for this dish as they are delicious, and high in protein.

Cut the yellow melon in half and discard the seeds. Scoop the flesh from one half with a Parisienne cutter to form neat balls. Arrange these on the plates. Cover the plates with clingfilm and chill while you make the dressing.

Scoop all the remaining melon flesh — both red and yellow — into a blender. Add the port, oil and ginger (with a little of its syrup). Blend to a smooth liquid. Season to taste.

Place the mushrooms in a bowl and pour on the dressing. Leave to marinate for 15 minutes.

Remove the mushrooms with a slotted spoon and arrange a few on each plate. Drizzle a little more dressing over each plate, and serve at once.

Variations: For a more substantial salad, thin slices of goat's cheese or firm tofu could be arranged on the plates before serving, and wholemeal (whole wheat) bread could be offered.

LA SALADE DE MANGETOUTS AU CÉLERI

Mangetout (Snow) Pea and Celery Salad

Preparation time: 10 minutes
Cooking time: 1 minute

This crisp salad, with its piquant cheese dressing, is of the sort that graces the tables of the chic Paris bistros, where young people gather to argue about politics and the arts, just as they always have done.

Imperial (Metric)	American
For the dressing:	*For the dressing:*
1 oz (25g) blue cheese	$\frac{1}{4}$ cup blue cheese
3 fl oz (90ml) sherry vinegar	$\frac{1}{3}$ cup sherry vinegar
1 oz (25g) toasted hazelnuts	$\frac{1}{4}$ cup toasted hazelnuts
For the salad:	*For the salad:*
1 round lettuce heart	1 round lettuce heart
1 orange	1 orange
8 oz (225g) celery sticks	$1\frac{1}{2}$ cups celery stalks
2 apples	2 apples
1 lb (450g) mangetout peas	1 pound snow peas
2 oz (50g) sesame seeds, toasted	4 tablespoons sesame seeds, toasted
Sea salt	Sea salt
Freshly ground black pepper	Freshly ground black pepper

Place all the ingredients for the dressing in a blender and blend to a smooth cream. Set aside for the flavours to mingle and develop.

Separate the lettuce leaves. Wash and drain well, then arrange to cover four individual serving plates.

Peel the orange and arrange segments prettily at the edges of the plates.

Trim the celery to remove any fibrous pieces. Cut into thin slices and place a mound in the centre of each plate.

Core the apples and cut into thin slices. Arrange these decoratively to harmonize with the orange segments.

Bring a large pan of salted water to the boil. Top and tail the mangetout (snow) peas and then plunge them into the boiling water. Bring back to the boil and blanch for 1 minute only. Then drain the peas and rinse in cold water to keep their colour and stop them cooking further.

Arrange the pea pods on the plates in a border around the celery. Season the salad lightly and sprinkle with sesame seeds. Finally, drizzle a little of the dressing over the salad, serving the rest in a sauceboat. Serve at once, preferably while the peas are still warm.

LA SALADE DE NOUILLE AU FENOUIL

Pasta Salad with Fennel

Preparation time: 10 minutes
Cooking time: 15 minutes

Pasta makes an excellent and substantial salad dish. Choose whole wheat pasta for a dish rich in protein and fibre, although green noodles — if made with spinach and not food dye — are very good for you, too, and look charming for this dish.

Imperial (Metric)	American
For the dressing:	*For the dressing:*
2 fl oz (60ml) raspberry vinegar	¼ cup raspberry vinegar
3 oz (75g) silken tofu	⅓ cup silken tofu
1 oz (25g) flaked almonds	¼ cup slivered almonds
1 teaspoon Dijon mustard	1 teaspoon Dijon mustard
1 teaspoon clear honey	1 teaspoon clear honey
1 tablespoon hot water	1 tablespoon hot water
Sea salt	Sea salt
Freshly ground black pepper	Freshly ground black pepper
For the salad:	*For the salad:*
8 oz (225g) thin noodles	8 ounces thin noodles
1 small oak leaf lettuce	1 small oak leaf lettuce
1 small bunch corn salad	1 small bunch corn salad
1 small head fennel	1 small head fennel
2 fl oz (60ml) vegetable oil	¼ cup vegetable oil
1 small onion, chopped	1 small onion, chopped
4 oz (100g) button mushrooms	2 cups button mushrooms
2 oz (50g) grated Gruyère cheese	½ cup grated Gruyère cheese
Sea salt	Sea salt
Freshly ground black pepper	Freshly ground black pepper

Place all the ingredients for the dressing in a blender and blend to a smooth cream. Check seasoning and set aside for the flavours to develop and mingle.

Bring a large pan of water to the boil and add the noodles. Bring back to the boil and simmer for 10 minutes (less if the noodles are fresh) or until the noodles are *al dente*.

Wash and drain the salad leaves and arrange around the edge of four serving plates. Thinly slice the fennel and set aside.

Heat the oil in a pan and sauté the onion gently for 3 minutes. Thinly slice the mushrooms and add them to the pan. Cook briefly so that they are just starting to soften.

Drain the noodles well and then add to the pan. Sprinkle with cheese and seasoning. Toss so that the noodles are mixed well with the vegetables and cheese.

Pile the noodles into the centre of each plate and garnish with thin slices of fennel. Serve, with the dressing offered separately.

LA SALADE MÉRIDIONALE AUX AUBERGINES

Spicy Aubergine (Eggplant) Salad

Preparation time: 5 minutes, plus 12 minutes soaking time
Cooking time: 4 minutes

Imperial (Metric)	American
For the dressing:	*For the dressing:*
2 tablespoons sherry vinegar	2 tablespoons sherry vinegar
2 fl oz (60ml) olive oil	$\frac{1}{4}$ cup olive oil
2 tablespoons peanut butter	2 tablespoons peanut butter
1 oz (25g) stuffed olives	$\frac{1}{4}$ cup stuffed olives
1 oz (25g) silken tofu	2 tablespoons silken tofu
2 cloves garlic, chopped	2 cloves garlic, chopped
1 tablespoon hot water	1 tablespoon hot water
Sea salt	Sea salt
Freshly ground black pepper	Freshly ground black pepper
For the salad:	*For the salad:*
1 large aubergine	1 large eggplant
Sea salt	Sea salt
2 oz (50g) soya flour	$\frac{1}{4}$ cup soy flour
1 free-range egg, beaten	1 free-range egg, beaten
1 oz (25g) desiccated coconut	$\frac{1}{3}$ cup desiccated coconut
1 red pepper	1 red pepper
1 green pepper	1 green pepper
4 'beefsteak' tomatoes	4 'beefsteak' tomatoes
1 red onion	1 red onion
1 large lettuce	1 large lettuce
Vegetable oil, for frying	Vegetable oil, for frying
8 stoned black olives	8 pitted black olives
2 tablespoons chopped coriander leaves	2 tablespoons chopped coriander leaves

Place all the dressing ingredients in a blender and blend to a smooth purée. Set aside for the flavours to develop and mingle.

Slice the aubergine (eggplant) into 8 thick diagonal pieces. Sprinkle with salt and leave for the juices to soak up for 12 minutes. Wash and pat dry. Pass the slices through the flour, then the egg, then coat in coconut and set aside.

De-seed the peppers and shred finely. Slice the tomatoes and onion across into circles. Separate the lettuce leaves, wash well and drain.

Arrange a bed of lettuce on a large serving plate, and then sprinkle with peppers and onion. Arrange the tomato slices around the edge.

Heat the oil in a large, shallow frying pan and sauté the aubergine (eggplant) slices until golden and sizzling on both sides. Transfer them straight from the pan onto the bed of lettuce, drizzle with a little dressing, sprinkle with olives and chopped coriander, and serve at once.

LA SALADE CATALANE

Exotic Rice Salad from Southern France

Serves: 8
Preparation time: 10 minutes
Cooking time: 25 minutes

Cooked peas and beans combine with the rice to make a complete protein in this main-course salad.

Imperial (Metric)	American
For the dressing:	*For the dressing:*
1 tablespoon French mustard	1 tablespoon French mustard
3 tablespoons olive oil	3 tablespoons olive oil
3 tablespoons sherry vinegar	3 tablespoons sherry vinegar
4 leaves tarragon	4 leaves tarragon
4 sprigs parsley	4 sprigs parsley
1 oz (25g) peanut butter	2 tablespoons peanut butter
Sea salt	Sea salt
Freshly ground black pepper	Freshly ground black pepper
For the salad:	*For the salad:*
2 fl oz (60ml) olive oil	¼ cup olive oil
1 small onion, chopped	1 small onion, chopped
4 cloves garlic, chopped	4 cloves garlic, chopped
8 oz (225g) brown rice	1 cup brown rice
1 teaspoon turmeric	1 teaspoon turmeric
1 round lettuce	1 round lettuce
4 firm tomatoes	4 firm tomatoes
1 small onion, sliced into rings	1 small onion, sliced into rings
2 oz (50g) cooked peas	⅓ cup cooked peas
2 oz (50g) diced red pepper	⅓ cup diced red pepper
2 oz (50g) diced green pepper	⅓ cup diced green pepper
2 oz (50g) cooked red kidney beans	⅓ cup cooked red kidney beans
4 stoned black olives	4 pitted black olives

Place all the dressing ingredients in a blender and blend to a smooth purée. Set aside for the flavours to develop and mingle.

Heat the oil in a pan and sauté the onion and garlic very briefly, then add the rice and stir-fry for a minute. Pour on 1¼ pints (700ml/3 cups) water.

When the water comes to the boil, tip the rice mixture into a large earthenware dish and cook in a preheated oven at 400°F/200°C (Gas Mark 6) until tender. When the rice is cooked, remove it from the oven and stir in the turmeric.

While the rice is cooking, wash the lettuce leaves and slice the tomatoes. Arrange a border of lettuce, tomato and onion rings around a large serving plate.

Once the rice is cooked, stir in the peas, peppers and kidney beans. Season to taste. Spoon the mixture into the centre of the serving plate. Splash with a little of the dressing, decorate with the halved olives, and serve while the rice is still warm.

LA SALADE POMME-POMME

Potato and Apple Salad

Preparation time: 10 minutes
Cooking time: 20 minutes

The pun in the title of this recipe stems from the French for apple — *pomme* — and that for potato — *pomme de terre* — whose names team up as well as do their flavours!

Imperial (Metric)	American
For the dressing:	*For the dressing:*
1 oz (25g) Roquefort cheese	¼ cup Roquefort cheese
3 fl oz (90ml) walnut oil	⅓ cup walnut oil
2 fl oz (60ml) cider vinegar	¼ cup cider vinegar
1 clove garlic, chopped	1 clove garlic, chopped
Juice and finely grated rind of	Juice and finely grated rind of
½ lemon	½ lemon
2 tablespoons fresh chopped	2 tablespoons fresh chopped
parsley	parsley
Sea salt	Sea salt
Freshly ground black pepper	Freshly ground black pepper
For the salad:	*For the salad:*
8 oz (225g) new potatoes	8 ounces new season potatoes
¼ white cabbage	¼ head white cabbage
1 onion, cut into thin rings	1 onion, cut into thin rings
1 sharp cooking apple	1 sharp cooking apple
2 oz (50g) chopped walnuts	½ cup chopped walnuts
2 tablespoons fresh chopped	2 tablespoons fresh chopped
parsley	parsley

Place all the dressing ingredients in a blender and blend until smooth. Check seasoning and set aside to allow the flavours to mingle and develop.

Bring a pan of salted water to the boil and cook the potatoes for 20 minutes, until tender.

While the potatoes are cooking, slice the cabbage and toss in half the dressing. Leave to marinate for 10 minutes, then arrange a ring of cabbage on each of four serving plates.

Drain the potatoes and slice. Toss in the remaining dressing and pile into the centre of the cabbage rings.

Sprinkle with onion rings. Core and thinly slice the apple and arrange around the plates. Sprinkle with walnuts and parsley. Serve at once.

AVOCAT ET CONCOMBRE, SAUCE MENTHE

Avocado and Cucumber Salad in a Mint Dressing

Preparation time: 10 minutes

To end this chapter of warm salads, here is an 'outsider' — a deliciously cool salad to refresh you on a hot summer's day.

Imperial (Metric)	American
For the salad:	*For the salad:*
2 ripe avocados	**2 ripe avocados**
1 cucumber	**1 cucumber**
1 head curly endive	**1 head curly chicory**
For the dressing:	*For the dressing:*
2 oz (50g) cucumber skin	**½ cup cucumber skin**
6 leaves mint	**6 leaves mint**
2 cloves garlic, chopped	**2 cloves garlic, chopped**
3 oz (75g) silken tofu	**⅓ cup silken tofu**
Juice of 1 lemon	**Juice of 1 lemon**
Sea salt	**Sea salt**
Freshly ground black pepper	**Freshly ground black pepper**

Halve, peel and slice the avocados. Peel and slice the cucumber, reserving sufficient skin for the dressing. Separate, wash and drain the salad leaves, and use them to make a pretty bed on a serving plate.

Arrange the slices of avocado and cucumber on the bed of leaves.

Place all the dressing ingredients in a blender and blend to a smooth cream. Adjust the consistency with a little water, if the cream is too thick.

Drizzle an attractive ribbon of dressing over the salad and serve.

Variations: The dressing could be spooned onto individual plates in a little pool, before the slices of avocado and cucumber are arranged over it. The plates can then be garnished with fronds of endive (chicory).

Chapter 4
LES PETITES ENTRÉES CHAUDES

Hot, Light Appetizers

The appetizer is an essential course for any dinner party meal, but its use should really be broader than that. Since it is — as its name implies — a dish intended to whet the appetite for further treats in store, it should be a light dish. If you feel even a little full after the appetizer, it was too heavy a dish, or your portion was too large.

So an appetizer can have a place in even a small, family meal. These days, as more and more people are cutting back their intake of sugary foods, perhaps more emphasis should be placed on a two-course meal of appetizer and main course, instead of main course and pudding.

Indeed, the wise businesswoman has revolutionized the traditional, heavy business lunch of her male predecessors by choosing two appetizers from the menu of even the most formal restaurants. And now some clever and forward-looking restaurateurs have created menus of appetizers *only*!

You will find dishes in this chapter that could be put to just such a use. Many need only the accompaniment of a salad, or a lightly steamed vegetable, or a fresh whole wheat roll, to make them into a healthy main course — especially since many dishes make good use of high-protein foods like soya (soy) flour and milk to provide excellent nourishment within the framework of a feather-light morsel of delicious food.

Remember simply that the perfect appetizer neither dulls the palate nor the appetite and this chapter will provide you with a wealth of choice and ideas to help start your meal off in perfect style.

CROQUE-EN-BOUCHE À LA PURÉE D'OLIVES ET DE NOIX

Choux Buns Stuffed with an Olive and Nut Cream

Preparation time: 5 minutes
Cooking time: 30 minutes

Once you have discovered just how easy it is to make choux pastry you will be amazed by its versatility. Try this elegant savoury appetizer as an introduction.

Imperial (Metric)	American
For the choux pastry:	*For the choux pastry:*
4 fl oz (120ml) water	½ cup water
2 oz (50g) butter	¼ cup butter
4 oz (100g) wholemeal flour	1 cup whole wheat flour
3 small free-range eggs, beaten	3 small free-range eggs, beaten
Sea salt	Sea salt
Freshly ground black pepper	Freshly ground black pepper
For the filling:	*For the filling:*
2 oz (50g) stuffed olives	½ cup stuffed olives
2 oz (50g) chopped walnuts	½ cup chopped walnuts
2 oz (50g) cream cheese	¼ cup cream cheese
1 tablespoon chopped parsley	1 tablespoon chopped parsley
1 chopped hard-boiled free-range egg	1 chopped hard-cooked free-range egg
Sea salt	Sea salt
Freshly ground black pepper	Freshly ground black pepper
For the croquant:	*For the croquant:*
1 oz (25g) clear honey	1 tablespoon clear honey
3 oz (75g) crushed salted peanuts	½ cup crushed salted peanuts

Place the water and butter in a large pan and heat until the fat melts and the water boils. Tip in the flour all at once, beating as you do so. Keep beating until the mixture forms a stiff paste that does not cling to the sides of the pan.

Remove from the heat and gradually beat in the egg until the paste forms a thick dropping consistency. Season lightly.

Place the mixture in a piping bag with a plain ¼ inch (6mm) nozzle. Onto a lightly oiled baking sheet, pipe 16 plum-sized blobs of the paste.

Bake the choux buns in a preheated oven at 400°F/200°C (Gas Mark 6) for 25 minutes, on the middle shelf.

While the buns are cooking, mince together all the filling ingredients to form a paste. If the mixture seems very thick, a little cream could be beaten in.

When the buns are puffed and golden, remove them from the oven and cool on a rack. Make a slit in the side of each, so that the filling can be inserted. Fill each bun, piping the filling in if necessary.

Dip one side of each bun in a very little honey, and then in crushed peanuts. Pile the buns onto a serving plate. Serve with slices of apple or pear for extra piquancy.

COURGETTES FARÇIES AUX MOUSSERONS

Stuffed Courgettes (Zucchini)

Preparation time: 5 minutes
Cooking time: 15 minutes

Mousserons à la Crème is a traditional Burgundian dish, a variation of which is used here as a filling for tender-crisp courgettes (zucchini).

Imperial (Metric)	American
4 large courgettes	4 large zucchini
2 oz (50g) butter	$\frac{1}{4}$ cup butter
1 shallot, chopped	1 shallot, chopped
2 cloves garlic, crushed	2 cloves garlic, crushed
4 oz (100g) chopped button mushrooms	$1\frac{1}{3}$ cups chopped button mushrooms
4 oz (100g) cooked, drained and chopped spinach	1 cup cooked, drained and chopped spinach
4 oz (100g) cream cheese	$\frac{1}{2}$ cup cream cheese
1 tablespoon tomato purée	1 tablespoon tomato paste
Sea salt	Sea salt
Freshly ground black pepper	Freshly ground black pepper
1 teaspoon honey	1 teaspoon honey
1 free-range egg, beaten	1 free-range egg, beaten
2 oz (50g) chopped pistachio nuts	$\frac{1}{2}$ cup chopped pistachio nuts

Trim the ends of the courgettes (zucchini), halve them lengthwise, and scoop out some of the flesh to form hollow 'boats'.

Bring a large pan of salted water to the boil and blanch the courgettes (zucchini) for 2 minutes. Drain well, then place in a buttered earthenware dish.

Heat the butter in a pan and sauté the shallot and garlic for 2 minutes. Add the mushrooms and spinach and cook gently for 4 minutes, to drive off any liquid.

Beat the cream cheese into the mixture, then the tomato purée (paste). Season to taste, and stir in the honey.

Remove the pan from the heat and beat in the egg and chopped nuts.

Fill the courgettes (zucchini) with this mixture, then place the dish in a preheated oven at 400°F/200°C (Gas Mark 6) for 5 minutes to reheat. Serve hot, with a salad of thinly sliced tomatoes and perhaps a dressing of yogurt and watercress.

CHAMPIGNONS DE PARIS À LA MOUTARDE

Mushrooms in a Creamy Mustard Sauce

Preparation time: 5 minutes, plus 10 minutes marinating time
Cooking time: 10 minutes

In the days before Les Halles was a fashionable shopping centre it was the central vegetable market for all of Paris. The tiny white mushrooms that were sold there, still fresh with dew from the fields, are always known in France as *champignons de Paris*. Now, of course, they are frequently cultivated indoors.

Imperial (Metric)	American
1 lb (450g) button mushrooms	1 pound button mushrooms
Juice of 1 lemon	Juice of 1 lemon
2 tablespoons brandy	2 tablespoons brandy
2 fl oz (60ml) sunflower oil	¼ cup sunflower oil
1 small shallot, chopped	1 small shallot, chopped
2 tablespoons sour cream	2 tablespoons sour cream
2 tablespoons tomato purée	2 tablespoons tomato paste
2 teaspoons honey	2 teaspoons honey
Sea salt	Sea salt
Freshly ground black pepper	Freshly ground black pepper
Small pinch cayenne pepper	Small pinch cayenne pepper
2 tablespoons Dijon mustard	2 tablespoons Dijon mustard
1 tablespoon wholemeal breadcrumbs	1 tablespoon whole wheat breadcrumbs
2 tablespoons grated cheese	2 tablespoons grated cheese

Clean the mushroms and trim the ends if sandy or damaged. (Ideally all the mushrooms should be small, and of roughly equal size.)

Place the mushrooms in a bowl and stir in the lemon juice and brandy. Leave to marinate for 10 minutes.

Heat the oil in a frying pan and sauté the shallot for 1 minute without browning. Pour in the juices from the mushrooms and reduce for 2 minutes.

Add the mushrooms to the pan and cook for 2 minutes. Remove them from the pan with a slotted spoon and keep warm in a shallow ovenproof dish.

Stir the cream, tomato purée (paste), honey and seasoning into the pan juices and boil for 2 minutes to reduce further. Last, stir in the mustard but do not allow the sauce to reboil.

Stir the sauce into the mushrooms. Mix together the breadcrumbs and cheese, and sprinkle this mixture over the dish. Brown under the grill (broiler) until golden. Serve with triangles of toasted whole wheat bread.

BRIOCHIN DE CHAMPIGNONS AUX HERBES

Field Mushroom Brioche

Preparation time: 10 minutes, plus 45 minutes proving time
Cooking time: 35 minutes

The delicious brioche bun is catching on in the rest of the world as quickly
as its cousin the croissant did a few years ago!

Imperial (Metric)	American
For the brioche:	*For the brioche:*
8 oz (225g) wholemeal flour	2 cups whole wheat flour
2 oz (50g) crushed peanuts	$\frac{1}{3}$ cup crushed peanuts
$\frac{1}{2}$ oz (15g) fresh yeast	1 tablespoon fresh yeast
2 fl oz (60ml) warm water	$\frac{1}{4}$ cup warm water
2 free-range eggs, beaten	2 free-range eggs, beaten
Sea salt	Sea salt
2 oz (50g) wholemeal flour for dusting the dough	$\frac{1}{2}$ cup whole wheat flour for dusting the dough
For the filling:	*For the filling:*
8 oz (225g) field mushrooms	4 cups flat mushrooms
2 fl oz (60ml) peanut oil	$\frac{1}{4}$ cup peanut oil
1 small onion, chopped	1 small onion, chopped
2 cloves garlic, crushed	2 cloves garlic, crushed
4 oz (100g) diced cooked potato	$\frac{2}{3}$ cup diced cooked potato
4 tablespoons mixed fresh chopped herbs of choice	4 tablespoons mixed fresh chopped herbs of choice
Sea salt	Sea salt
Freshly ground black pepper	Freshly ground black pepper

In a large bowl, combine the flour and peanuts. In a smaller bowl, dissolve
the yeast in the water, then beat in the eggs. Season with a little salt.

Pour the liquid into the flour, beating to form a smooth dough. Gather the
dough into a ball, cover with a damp cloth and leave to prove for 30
minutes. It should double in size. Punch the dough down again, knead
briefly, then prove again for 15 minutes.

While the dough is resting, make the filling. First, trim, clean and slice the
mushrooms.

Heat the oil in a pan and sauté the onion and garlic until translucent. Add the mushrooms and cook for 3 minutes. Mix in the potato and herbs. Season to taste and remove from the heat to cool slightly.

Punch down the dough again and roll out to an oblong, 12 by 7 inches (30 by 18cm) and about $\frac{1}{4}$ inch (5mm) thick. Lay this on a lightly greased baking tray.

Spoon the filling into the centre of the dough, then bring the dough up over it. Pinch and tuck in the edges to seal in the filling, then turn the sausage shape over to form a loaf. Brush the top with a little milk.

Bake at 425°F/220°C (Gas Mark 7) on the middle shelf for 30 minutes. Allow to cool, then slice and serve with avocado and tomato salad.

BRANDADE DE POMMES ET D'HARICOTS SOISSONNAIS

Potato and Bean Fritters with Tomato Coulis

Preparation time: 10 minutes
Cooking time: 12 minutes

This tasty dish makes an original use of left-over potatoes and cooked beans. Soissons in France is renowned for its haricot beans, which are so tender that they need no soaking before they can be cooked.

Imperial (Metric)	*American*
1 tablespoon chopped onion	1 tablespoon chopped onion
2 cloves garlic, chopped	2 cloves garlic, chopped
2 tablespoons peanut oil	2 tablespoons peanut oil
8 oz (225g) cooked potato, mashed	1 cup cooked potato, mashed
4 oz (100g) cooked haricot beans, mashed	$\frac{2}{3}$ cup cooked haricot beans, mashed
2 oz (50g) cream cheese	$\frac{1}{4}$ cup cream cheese
$\frac{1}{2}$ recipe choux pastry dough (page 72)	$\frac{1}{2}$ recipe choux pastry dough (page 72)
Vegetable oil for frying	Vegetable oil for frying
For the coulis:	*For the coulis:*
$\frac{1}{2}$ red pepper, seeded	$\frac{1}{2}$ red pepper, seeded
1 large 'beefsteak' tomato	1 'beefsteak' tomato
1 clove garlic, crushed	1 clove garlic, crushed
1 teaspoon cornflour	1 teaspoon cornstarch
3 tablespoons water	3 tablespoons water
Sea salt	Sea salt
Freshly ground black pepper	Freshly ground black pepper
1 teaspoon honey	1 teaspoon honey
Juice of $\frac{1}{2}$ a lemon (optional)	Juice of $\frac{1}{2}$ a lemon (optional)

Purée the onion, garlic and peanut oil in a blender, then beat this mixture into the mashed potato. Into this, mix the mashed beans and the cream cheese.

Blend this mixture into the prepared choux pastry dough.

Shape this mixture into small egg-shapes and set aside while you make the coulis.

Dice the red pepper finely. Skin and deseed the tomato. Place in a pan with the garlic and heat gently for 3 minutes, stirring, to cook lightly.

Mix together the starch and water. Stir this into the pan and cook for a further 4 minutes until thickened and cooked. Place the contents of the pan in a blender and purée until smooth. Season to taste and stir in the honey. Lemon juice may be added if wished, but do not make the sauce too thin. Place the sauce in a pan to reheat.

Heat the oil in a deep pan and drop in three or four brandades at a time to cook. When they float on the surface, puffed and golden, they are cooked. Keep warm on kitchen paper towels until all are cooked.

Pour a pool of coulis onto each serving plate and arrange the brandades on this. Serve at once.

CASSOLETTE D'AUBERGINE MARTINIQUE

Baked Aubergine (Eggplant) Custards

Preparation time: 10 minutes, plus 15 minutes soaking time
Cooking time: 25 to 30 minutes

The delicately flavoured custard in this dish balances the richness of the aubergine (eggplant) slices. Serve with a tangy tomato *coulis* for an attractive and appetizing first course.

Imperial (Metric)	American
1 medium aubergine	1 medium eggplant
Sea salt	Sea salt
1 oz (25g) seasoned wholemeal flour	¼ cup seasoned whole wheat flour
4 free-range eggs, beaten	4 free-range eggs, beaten
1 oz (25g) desiccated coconut	⅓ cup desiccated coconut
3 fl oz (90ml) sunflower oil	⅓ cup sunflower oil
¼ pint (150ml) single cream	⅔ cup light cream
Freshly ground black pepper	Freshly ground black pepper
Pinch freshly ground nutmeg	Pinch freshly ground nutmeg
1 tablespoon chopped onion	1 tablespoon chopped onion
1 clove garlic, crushed	1 clove garlic, crushed

Slice the aubergine (eggplant) into 8 evenly thick rounds. Sprinkle with salt and leave for the bitter juices to soak out. After 15 minutes, rinse and drain. Pat dry with a clean cloth.

Spread the flour on a clean plate, half the beaten egg on another, and the coconut on a third. Pass each slice through each in turn.

Heat the oil in a large frying pan and sauté each slice for 30 seconds on each side to lightly brown. Lay a slice in the base of four individual ramekins.

Beat the cream into the remaining beaten egg. Season and add nutmeg.

In the pan used to cook the aubergine (eggplant), sauté the onion and garlic briefly. Stir this into the egg and cream. Fill the ramekins with this mixture.

Top each ramekin with another slice of aubergine (eggplant).

Place the ramekins in a baking tray, and pour hot water in to come half way up the sides of the ramekins. Place the baking tray in a preheated oven at 400°F/200°C (Gas Mark 6) and cook for 20 to 25 minutes. Turn out the cooked custards onto the sauce of your choice and serve at once.

TOMATES RIVIÉRA

Tomatoes Stuffed with Goat's Cheese, Nuts and Garlic

Preparation time: 15 minutes
Cooking time: 5 to 8 minutes

Baked stuffed tomatoes have a tendency to be insipid, but this rich and flavoursome filling ensures that this is not the case here.

Imperial (Metric)	American
4 large tomatoes	4 large tomatoes
2 oz (50g) chopped walnuts	½ cup chopped walnuts
1 oz (25g) wholemeal breadcrumbs	½ cup whole wheat breadcrumbs
2 cloves garlic, crushed	2 cloves garlic, crushed
2 oz (50g) goat's cheese	½ cup goat's cheese
1 tablespoon chopped fresh herbs	1 tablespoon chopped fresh herbs
1 free-range egg, beaten	1 free-range egg, beaten
Sea salt	Sea salt
Freshly ground black pepper	Freshly ground black pepper

Trim the stem end of each tomato, then turn upside down and cut one-third off the base of each one (they will be cooked and served stemside down, as this makes for a steadier base).

Scoop out all the pulp, discarding seeds where possible but reserving the flesh in a bowl. Place the tomato shells upside-down to drain while the filling is prepared.

Place the walnuts, breadcrumbs and garlic in a bowl, then mash in the cheese. Add the herbs, then blend in the egg. Season to taste. Stir the chopped tomato pulp into the mixture and ensure that everything is well mixed.

Fill the tomato shells with the mixture, then stand in a shallow baking dish. Bake at 450°F/230°C (Gas Mark 8) for 5 to 8 minutes, so that the filling is cooked but the tomatoes have not had time to collapse or split. Serve at once.

SOUFFLETON D'ÉPINARD À LA NOIX DE COCO

Spinach and Coconut Soufflé

Serves: 8
Preparation time: 10 minutes
Cooking time: 25 to 30 minutes

This light, protein-rich little soufflé makes an elegant appetizer to a meal, or a sophisticated luncheon dish if served with a tomato and shallot salad for contrasting flavours, textures and colour.

Imperial (Metric)	American
4 oz (100g) polyunsaturated margarine	½ cup polyunsaturated margarine
1 oz (25g) toasted desiccated coconut	⅓ cup toasted desiccated coconut
Scant 2oz (50g) wholemeal flour	Scant ½ cup whole wheat flour
1 tablespoon soya flour	1 tablespoon soy flour
¾ pint (425ml) soya milk	2 cups soy milk
1 free-range egg, beaten	1 free-range egg, beaten
2 free-range egg yolks	2 free-range egg yolks
2 oz (50g) dry spinach purée	¼ cup dry spinach purée
2 oz (50g) crushed walnuts	½ cup crushed walnuts
Sea salt	Sea salt
Freshly ground black pepper	Freshly ground black pepper
Freshly grated nutmeg	Freshly grated nutmeg
3 free-range egg whites	3 free-range egg whites

Use half the margarine to grease 8 small ramekins, then coat the insides with coconut. Set aside.

Heat the remaining margarine in a pan and cook the flours gently to make a roux.

Gradually add the milk to the roux, stirring in well to avoid lumps. When you have achieved a creamy white sauce, remove the pan from the heat and beat in the beaten egg and the egg yolks.

Return the pan to the heat and reboil the sauce until it is just bubbling. Remove from the heat again and beat in the spinach, nuts and seasoning.

In a very clean bowl, whisk the egg whites with a pinch of salt until they form stiff peaks. Mix one third of this into the sauce mixture, then lightly fold in the remaining egg whites a little at a time.

Fill the ramekins to the top with the mixture. Run the back of a teaspoon around the edge of the mixture, so that the tops of the soufflés will rise well.

Preheat the oven to 400°F/200°C (Gas Mark 6). Place the ramekins in a baking tray and pour hot water in to come half way up the sides of the ramekins. Bake for 20 to 25 minutes, until the soufflés are well-risen and golden. Serve at once.

FOURNÉE DE CHOUX DE BRUXELLES DE FRÉVENT

Country Sprout and Chestnut Omelette

Preparation time: 10 minutes
Cooking time: 10 minutes

This dish — minus its garnish of pawpaw/papaya — was a traditional miner's supper in the village where my father was born but, with a few modern variations, it makes a tasty appetizer.

Imperial (Metric)	American
2 fl oz (60ml) sunflower oil	¼ cup sunflower oil
2 oz (50g) chopped cooked chestnuts	½ cup chopped cooked chestnuts
3 oz (75g) chopped cooked Brussels sprouts	½ cup chopped cooked Brussels sprouts
1 medium onion, chopped	1 medium onion, chopped
3 flat mushrooms, sliced	3 flat mushrooms, sliced
1 clove garlic, crushed	1 clove garlic, crushed
½ teaspoon mustard seeds	½ teaspoon mustard seeds
3 free-range eggs, beaten	3 free-range eggs, beaten
1 teaspoon wholemeal flour	1 teaspoon whole wheat flour
Sea salt	Sea salt
Freshly ground black pepper	Freshly ground black pepper
2 oz (50g) curd cheese	¼ cup curd cheese
½ pawpaw, peeled and sliced	½ papaya, peeled and sliced
2 oz (50g) grated cheese	½ cup grated cheese

Heat the oil in a frying pan and sauté all the vegetables, together with the mustard seeds, for 4 minutes until cooked but not browned.

Beat together the eggs, flour and seasoning, then pour this mixture into the pan. Stir and cook, as you would an omelette, and when it is cooked through, slip the omelette onto greaseproof (parchment) paper.

Spread the omelette with the curd cheese and roll it up. Place it in an earthenware dish and flatten it slightly. Arrange slices of pawpaw (papaya) around the edge, and sprinkle cheese over the dish.

Brown the cheese under a hot grill (broiler) for a couple of minutes, then cut the omelette into slices and serve with the pawpaw (papaya) garnish.

RAGÔUT DE LÉGUMES À LA PÉRIGOURDINE

Vegetable Stew with Truffle

Preparation time: 15 minutes
Cooking time: 40 minutes

The Périgord region is famed for its truffles, and even the smallest amount certainly lends a magical quality to even the simplest dishes. But if truffles are beyond your reach, sautéed field mushrooms can replace them quite happily in this good country stew.

Imperial (Metric)	American
4 medium onions, sliced	4 medium onions, sliced
2 oz (50g) butter	¼ cup butter
2 lb (900g) small potatoes, sliced	2 pounds small potatoes, sliced
1 lb (450g) turnips, peeled and sliced	1 pound turnips, peeled and sliced
4 fl oz (120ml) vegetable stock	½ cup vegetable stock
4 juniper berries	4 juniper berries
Sea salt	Sea salt
Freshly ground black pepper	Freshly ground black pepper
4 large tomatoes, skinned, seeded and chopped	4 large tomatoes, skinned, seeded and chopped
2 fl oz (60ml) olive or walnut oil	¼ cup olive or walnut oil
1 small truffle, chopped	1 small truffle, chopped
4 oz (100g) grated cheese	1 cup grated cheese

Lightly sauté the onions in the butter until just soft, then lay in the base of an ovenproof earthenware dish. Cover with layers of potatoes and turnips.

Pour the stock over the dish, add the juniper berries and season to taste.

Cover the dish with chopped tomatoes and drizzle with oil. Place the dish in the oven and bake at 400°F/200°C (Gas Mark 6) for 35 minutes. The dish is cooked when the vegetables are tender when prodded with a knife or skewer.

Sprinkle the dish with chopped truffle and then grated cheese. Place under a hot grill (broiler) or return to the oven to brown. Serve at once.

Note: Instead of truffles, substitute 2 oz (50g/1 cup) sliced mushrooms, sautéed briefly in a knob of butter.

TIMBALE DE MOUSSAKA DU SULTAN

Moussaka Timbales

Preparation time: 10 minutes
Cooking time: 40 minutes

Moussaka is usually made with minced lamb, but since it is the wonderful aubergine (eggplant) that we truly associate with this dish, here is a variation that is elegant and quintessentially exotic.

Imperial (Metric)	American
1 aubergine	1 eggplant
Sea salt	Sea salt
1 free-range egg, beaten	1 free-range egg, beaten
1 oz (25g) wholemeal flour	$\frac{1}{4}$ cup wholemeal flour
1 oz (25g) desiccated coconut	$\frac{1}{4}$ cup desiccated coconut
2 fl oz (60ml) olive oil	$\frac{1}{4}$ cup olive oil
1 oz (25g) chopped onion	$\frac{1}{4}$ cup chopped onion
2 cloves garlic, crushed	2 cloves garlic, crushed
4 oz (100g) soft goat's cheese	$\frac{1}{2}$ cup soft goat's cheese
2 free-range eggs, beaten	2 free-range eggs, beaten
1 tablespoon chopped fresh coriander	1 tablespoon chopped fresh coriander
Freshly ground black pepper	Freshly ground black pepper
1 recipe hot Tomato Coulis (page 80)	1 recipe hot Tomato Coulis (page 80)

Thinly slice the aubergine (eggplant) and sprinkle with salt. Leave to drain off the bitter juices, then wash well and pat dry. Pass the slices through a mixture of flour and coconut.

Heat the oil in a shallow pan and sauté the aubergine (eggplant) slices briefly on both sides. Drain on kitchen paper towels.

In the remaining oil (or add a little more, if necessary), sauté the onion and garlic until tender. Drain off the oil and beat the onion and garlic into the cheese. Beat in the eggs, then the fresh coriander. Season to taste.

Lightly grease 4 dariole moulds, then line with slices of aubergine (eggplant), reserving 4 slices of a suitable size to cover the tops of the moulds. Fill with cheese mixture, then cover with the reserved slices.

Place the moulds in a bain marie and bake at 400°F/200°C (Gas Mark 6) for 30 to 35 minutes, until set. Serve unmoulded over a pool of hot Tomato Coulis (page 80) — leave the moussaka moulds to stand for 12 minutes before turning them out, since the moussaka should be served warm, in the Greek tradition.

LES JEUX D'AMOUR

Tomato and Apple Charlotte

Preparation time: 10 minutes
Cooking time: 26 minutes

The tomato was known as the 'love apple' when it was first introduced into Europe, because it was thought to be an aphrodisiac! Here it is teamed with real apples in a dish which is pretty enough to win hearts!

Imperial (Metric)	American
2 oz (50g) unsalted butter	$\frac{1}{4}$ cup sweet butter
1 oz (25g) finely crushed peanuts	2 tablespoons finely crushed peanuts
4 Cox's apples	4 sharp eating apples
4 large ribbed tomatoes	4 large ribbed tomatoes
4 oz (100g) silken tofu	$\frac{1}{2}$ cup silken tofu
4 free-range eggs, beaten	4 free-range eggs, beaten
1 oz (25g) wholemeal breadcrumbs	$\frac{1}{2}$ cup whole wheat breadcrumbs
4 leaves fresh basil	4 leaves fresh basil
Sea salt	Sea salt
Freshly ground black pepper	Freshly ground black pepper

Grease four dariole moulds with the butter and coat with crushed peanuts.

Peel, core and slice the apples. Blanch in boiling salted water for 1 minute, then drain well.

Skin, seed and slice the tomatoes.

Arrange alternate layers of apple and tomato slices in the moulds, but do not fill more than three-quarters full.

In a bowl, mash together the tofu and the beaten eggs. Stir in the breadcrumbs. Chop the basil leaves finely and add to the mixture. Season.

Spoon the mixture into the dariole moulds, making sure that it runs down amongst the layers of apple and tomato.

Place the moulds in a baking tray, and pour in hot water to come half way up the sides of the moulds.

Bake in a preheated oven at 400°F/200°C (Gas Mark 6) for 25 minutes. Cool slightly before unmoulding onto serving plates. This dish looks very charming served on a purée of cooked spinach flavoured with a little lemon juice.

NAVET NIVERNAIS AU VERT

Stuffed Turnip on a Bed of Broccoli

Preparation time: 10 minutes
Cooking time: 25 minutes

This frivolous appetizer reflects the good vegetable produce of the rolling countryside of the Nivernais region of Burgundy.

Imperial (Metric)	American
4 medium turnips	4 medium turnips
8 oz (225g) mashed potato	1 cup mashed potato
1 free-range egg, beaten	1 free-range egg, beaten
2 oz (50g) chopped walnuts	$\frac{1}{2}$ cup chopped walnuts
Sea salt	Sea salt
Freshly ground black pepper	Freshly ground black pepper
8 oz (225g) broccoli florets	3 cups broccoli florets
4 fl oz (120ml) natural yogurt	$\frac{1}{2}$ cup plain yogurt

Peel the turnips neatly to retain their shape. Blanch for 8 minutes in boiling salted water.

Scoop out the centres of the turnips with a Parisian cutter, and boil the centre flesh a little longer until soft.

Mash the soft turnip flesh and mix it into the mashed potato. Stir in the beaten egg, nuts and seasoning.

Fill a piping bag with the mixture and fill the centres of the turnip shells with the mixture. Pipe a little blob on the top, like a cottage loaf.

Meanwhile, boil the broccoli florets in salted water for 8 minutes. Drain and chop coarsely. Blend in the yogurt and season to taste.

Place a little of the broccoli mixture in each of four small ovenproof dishes. In the centre of each, set a stuffed turnip. Bake in a preheated oven at 400°F/200°C (Gas Mark 6) for 10 minutes, to heat through. This is nice served with a sauce of cream and fresh mint, but is very good just as it is.

Chapter 5
LES PLATS DU JOUR

Dishes of the Day

In a restaurant the *plat du jour* is the special dish that is being featured, based on what was fresh and inexpensive in the market that morning. It is by no means a dish to be looked down on for this reason — indeed, by choosing the *plat du jour* you can be sure of a dish made fresh, from the freshest seasonal ingredients. Surely this is a treat to be anticipated!

It is also an approach to be followed when cooking for yourself and your family. In France, the market is a place to be visited daily. The French man or woman makes every effort to get to know the traders so that their advice about produce can be sought every time, and the advice is always honest and reliable — the stallholder will take pride in offering only the best to the discerning shopper. So the main meal for a French family is almost always a *plat du jour*, unlike the canned and frozen foods, year-in-year-out the very same, that so many other countries regard as staple food, to be bulk bought from the supermarket as a weekly or monthly chore.

We French do not often stint on the quality of our ingredients, regardless of cost. If we feel a dish will benefit from a special oil, such as walnut, we will purchase a bottle without flinching. If a truffle is what it takes to lift a simple dish into the realms of gustatory delight, then so be it. It seems to me especially reasonable as part of a vegetarian meal — after all, money is not being lavished on costly cuts of meat, so why should not a little of the money you save be allotted to the pleasures offered by the infinitely varied vegetable kingdom?

You will find in this chapter just a handful of my favourite *plats du jour*. The ideas I have suggested will no doubt spark off other possibilities in your mind. Don't forget that vegetables are very adaptable — if asparagus has just reached its peak when you visit the vegetable stall, it will not take much effort to substitute it for green beans in a recipe you wish to cook. One of the great maxims of the French is to shop first, and choose a recipe second. It is easy enough to do — far easier, in fact, than deciding to cook a dish requiring fresh garden peas, for instance, in April — and will ensure that you are getting the very best in terms of nutrients, flavour, texture *and* economy from your food.

CASSEROLE DE LÉGUMES AU CARVI

Vegetable Casserole with a Caraway Scone Topping

Serves: 6
Preparation time: 15 minutes
Cooking time: 45 minutes

This is a dish from Alsace, in Eastern France. It is good, substantial country fare that is best accompanied by the beer of that region.

Imperial (Metric)	American
2 fl oz (60ml) vegetable oil	¼ cup vegetable oil
2 onions, cut into thin strips	2 onions, cut into thin strips
2 cloves garlic, chopped	2 cloves garlic, chopped
1 green pepper, seeded and cut into thin strips	1 green pepper, seeded and cut into thin strips
1 red pepper, seeded and cut into thin strips	1 red pepper, seeded and cut into thin strips
4 carrots, scrubbed and sliced	4 carrots, scrubbed and sliced
2 parsnips, peeled and sliced	2 parsnips, peeled and sliced
¼ pint (150ml) dry white wine	⅔ cup dry white wine
¼ pint (150ml) water	⅔ cup water
1 tablespoon yeast extract	1 tablespoon yeast extract
Sea salt	Sea salt
Freshly ground black pepper	Freshly ground black pepper
For the scone topping:	*For the scone topping:*
8 oz (225g) wholemeal flour	2 cups whole wheat flour
2 teaspoons baking powder	2 teaspoons baking powder
Sea salt	Sea salt
1 teaspoon caraway seeds	1 teaspoon caraway seeds
2 oz (50g) polyunsaturated or vegan margarine	¼ cup polyunsaturated or vegan margarine
¼ pint (150ml) skimmed or soya milk	⅔ cup skim or soy milk

Heat the oil in a large pan and sauté all the vegetables for 2 minutes, then stir in the wine, water and yeast extract. Bring to the boil and then simmer for 20 minutes so that the vegetables are almost cooked and the sauce thickens. Taste and then season. Pour the mixture into an earthenware dish and keep warm.

Prepare the scones by sifting together the flour, baking powder and salt into a bowl. Add back any bran left behind, and stir in the caraway seeds.

Rub in the margarine, then mix in enough milk to make a smooth, firm dough (reserve at least 2 tablespoons of milk for glazing the scones).

Roll out the dough to $\frac{1}{2}$ inch (1cm) thick and cut 2-inch (5cm) circles with a pastry cutter or a wine glass. Lay the scone circles around the edge of the casserole dish, keeping the centre clear. Brush with a little milk.

Bake the casserole in a preheated oven at 400°F/200°C (Gas Mark 6) for 15 minutes, to heat the vegetable stew well and cook the scone topping. Serve at once.

OIGNONS BORDELAIS

Onions in Red Wine with Roasted Chick Peas

Preparation time: 15 minutes, plus soaking time
Cooking time: 25 minutes

The contrast of the little onions, simmered in a rich claret sauce, with the crunch of the roast chick peas, makes this simple dish a gastronomic treat.

Imperial (Metric)	American
8 oz (225g) chick peas	1 cup chick peas
1 lb (450g) baby onions	1 pound baby onions
2 fl oz (60ml) walnut oil	¼ cup walnut oil
2 cloves garlic, crushed	2 cloves garlic, crushed
2 tablespoons tomato purée	2 tablespoons tomato paste
2 tablespoons honey	2 tablespoons honey
1 teaspoon mixed spice	1 teaspoon mixed spice
8 fl oz (240ml) red Bordeaux wine	1 cup red Bordeaux wine
2 large tomatoes, skinned, seeded and diced	2 large tomatoes, skinned, seeded and diced
1 sprig thyme	1 sprig thyme
5 basil leaves	5 basil leaves
3 oz (75g) seedless raisins	½ cup seedless raisins
4 fl oz (120ml) water	½ cup water
Sea salt	Sea salt
Freshly ground black pepper	Freshly ground black pepper

Soak the chick peas in water for 8 hours, or overnight. Drain, rinse and drain again.

Peel the onions. Heat the oil in a large pan and sauté the onions until golden.

Add the garlic, tomato purée (paste), honey, spice and wine and boil until the wine has almost evaporated and the mixture is syrupy.

Stir in the tomatoes, herbs and raisins, then add the water to just come level with the other ingredients. Add seasoning and leave to simmer for 20 minutes.

Heat the oven to its hottest temperature. Place the drained chick peas on a baking tray and roast for about 12 minutes, moving them about frequently to ensure even cooking. They should be golden-brown, with a delicious nutty aroma but without a hint of scorching.

Spoon the cooked onions into the centre of a warmed serving dish and arrange the roasted chick peas around the edge. Serve with plain boiled brown rice or thick chunks of fresh whole wheat bread to mop up the juices.

OIGNON FARÇI AU ROQUEFORT

Baked Onions, Stuffed with Cheese and Nuts

Preparation time: 12 minutes
Cooking time: 1 hour

Here is another stuffed vegetable dish, which also makes use of pine kernels (pignoli) in the stuffing — although, since the cheese and bean mixture is quite rich in flavour, you could substitute peanuts for a cheaper but just as nourishing meal.

Imperial (Metric)	American
4 large onions, of equal size	4 large onions, of equal size
4 oz (100g) pine nuts or peanuts	¾ cup pignoli or peanuts
3 oz (75g) crumbled Roquefort	¾ cup crumbled Roquefort
1 oz (25g) wholemeal breadcrumbs	½ cup whole wheat breadcrumbs
3 oz (75g) cooked, mashed haricot beans	½ cup cooked, mashed navy beans
1 hard-boiled free-range egg, chopped	1 hard-cooked free-range egg, chopped
1 oz (25g) seedless raisins	2 tablespoons seedless raisins
Sea salt	Sea salt
Freshly ground black pepper	Freshly ground black pepper
Vegetable oil, for basting	Vegetable oil, for basting

Peel the onions and cut off the top quarter of each one. Plunge into boiling salted water and cook for 12 minutes. Drain and cool.

Squeeze out the centres of the onions, leaving just a couple of layers to hold the filling. Chop the inside layers and place them in a bowl.

Into the chopped onion, mix all the other ingredients except the oil. Mash well to form a firm, well-mixed paste. Fill the onions with this mixture, heaping the tops if necessary to use up all the filling.

Oil an ovenproof dish and place the onions in this. Bake at 350°F/180°C (Gas Mark 4) for 45 minutes, basting with oil from time to time. Serve each onion on a pool of Tomato Coulis (page 80), garnished with curly lettuce and slices of fresh peach or segments of grapefruit.

COMPOTE D'ÉPINARD AU COUSCOUS

Couscous with Spinach and Walnuts

Serves: 6
Preparation time: 10 minutes
Cooking time: 20 minutes

The cuisine of the South of France, especially around the port of Marseilles, has a cosmopolitan flavour reflecting trade with former colonies in Africa. Couscous is one of my favourite dishes of this type, and it is equally popular amongst young Parisians at the moment.

Imperial (Metric)	American
2 lb (900g) fresh spinach	2 pounds fresh spinach
2 fl oz (60ml) walnut oil	$\frac{1}{4}$ cup walnut oil
4 oz (100g) walnut kernels	$\frac{3}{4}$ cup walnut kernels
4 oz (100g) diced dried dates	$\frac{2}{3}$ cup diced dried dates
2 cloves garlic, chopped	2 cloves garlic, chopped
Juice of 1 lemon	Juice of 1 lemon
Sea salt	Sea salt
Freshly ground black pepper	Freshly ground black pepper
Freshly ground mace	Freshly ground mace
4 oz (100g) couscous	1 cup couscous
1 tablespoon olive oil	1 tablespoon olive oil
$\frac{1}{2}$ pint (300ml) water or vegetable stock	$1\frac{1}{3}$ cups water or vegetable stock
1 red or green chilli, seeded and sliced	1 red or green chili, seeded and sliced
Pinch ground cumin	Pinch ground cumin

Wash the spinach well, removing any coarse stems or damaged leaves. Heat the oil in a large pan and add the spinach. Cook, stirring, until the leaves wilt. Add the walnuts and dates. Blend the garlic with the lemon juice and stir this in. Cover and simmer for 15 minutes before seasoning.

Rub the couscous with the oil, then place in a pan and sauté for 1 minute. Pour in the water or stock, add the chilli, and cook for 5 minutes before transferring to an earthenware dish. Dry in a preheated oven at 400°F/200°C (Gas Mark 6) for 10 to 12 minutes, fluffing with a fork occasionally to separate the grains. Season with salt and cumin.

Make a ring of couscous on a warmed serving plate and pile the cooked spinach compote into the centre. Serve at once.

MÉLI-MÉLO D'HARICOTS AU YAOURT

Bean and Vegetable Stew with a Fruity Yogurt Garnish

Serves: 6
Preparation time: 15 minutes, plus soaking time
Cooking time: 2 hours

Here is an exciting combination — a simple stew of good old-fashioned beans and vegetables, mingled with exotic fruits and the piquant tang of yogurt.

Imperial (Metric)	American
12 oz (350g) haricot beans	1½ cups navy beans
2 small onions	2 small onions
4 cloves	4 cloves
2 carrots	2 carrots
2 cleaned leeks, white parts only	2 cleaned leeks, white parts only
3 cloves garlic, chopped	3 cloves garlic, chopped
8 small turnips	8 small turnips
1 ripe pawpaw	1 ripe papaya
1 slice pineapple	1 slice pineapple
1 small Charentais melon	1 small Charentais melon
¼ pint (150ml) natural yogurt	⅔ cup plain yogurt
Sea salt	Sea salt
Freshly ground black pepper	Freshly ground black pepper

Soak the beans for 8 hours, or overnight.

Peel the onions and stud with the cloves.

Rinse and drain the beans, then place in a pan with fresh distilled or bottled water. Add the onions. Bring to the boil, cover and simmer for 1½ hours, or until the beans are just tender. Skim off any scum as it rises.

Slice the leeks into large chunks, slice the carrots more thinly, and add these with the garlic to the pan. Cook for a further 20 minutes.

Peel and quarter the turnips and add to the pan. Cook for a further 8 minutes.

Peel, seed and chop the pawpaw (papaya), cube the pineapple, halve and seed the melon and scoop out the flesh.

Drain the bean and vegetable mixture of any remaining liquid. Allow to cool very slightly and then stir in the fruit and yogurt. Season to taste and serve at once on a bed of lettuce.

RATA MARSEILLAISE

Saffron-Scented Vegetable Casserole with Eggs

Serves: 6
Preparation time: 15 minutes
Cooking time: 25 minutes

Here is another dish from the region of Provence in southern France. You might be surprised to discover how such small amounts of saffron and basil are needed to give all the flavour, aroma and character of this region to the dish.

Imperial (Metric)	American
2 fl oz (60ml) olive oil	¼ cup olive oil
1 large onion, thinly sliced	1 large onion, thinly sliced
4 cloves garlic, chopped	4 cloves garlic, chopped
1 stick celery, chopped	1 stalk celery, chopped
1 stick fennel, chopped	1 stalk fennel, chopped
2 oz (50g) tomato purée	¼ cup tomato paste
1 pint (600ml) water	2½ cups water
1 lb (450g) new potatoes, scrubbed and quartered	1 pound new season potatoes, scrubbed and quartered
6 strands saffron	6 strands saffron
1 teaspoon turmeric	1 teaspoon turmeric
1 unsalted vegetable stock cube	1 unsalted vegetable stock cube
2 green chillis, seeded and sliced	2 green chilis, seeded and sliced
4 chopped basil leaves	4 chopped basil leaves
3 chopped mint leaves	3 chopped mint leaves
4 courgettes, thickly sliced	4 zucchini, thickly sliced
Sea salt	Sea salt
Freshly ground black pepper	Freshly ground black pepper
4 hard-boiled free-range eggs	4 hard-cooked free-range eggs

Heat the oil in a large pan and sauté the onion, garlic, celery and fennel for 3 minutes without browning. Add the tomato purée (paste) and water, and boil for 2 minutes before stirring in the potatoes.

Simmer for 15 minutes, then add the saffron, turmeric, stock cube, chillis, herbs and courgettes (zucchini).

Cook for a further 5 minutes, then taste and season. Halve the eggs, then lay some of the vegetable mixture in the base of a warmed earthenware serving dish. Lay the eggs, cut sides down, onto this and cover with the remaining vegetable mixture. Serve with a cooling salad as this dish is quite fiery.

Note: Vegans could substitute cubes of lightly sautéd smoked tofu for the eggs in this dish.

LE CLAFOUTU AUX AUBERGINES

Rich Aubergine (Eggplant) Pudding

Preparation time: 12 minutes
Cooking time: 55 minutes

All lovers of French cuisine will have heard of *Clafoutis*, but few will know how to make a *Clafoutu*. Well, here is my aunt Galibert's version of this dish as an introduction.

Imperial (Metric)	American
1 quince, cored, peeled and sliced	1 quince, cored, peeled and sliced
2 large aubergines, sliced	2 large eggplants, sliced
2 oz (50g) toasted crushed almonds	¼ cup toasted crushed almonds
2 fl oz (60ml) walnut oil	¼ cup walnut oil
4 cloves garlic, crushed	4 cloves garlic, crushed
1 large onion, sliced into rings	1 large onion, sliced into rings
1 large ribbed tomato	1 large ribbed tomato
2 oz (50g) softened butter	¼ cup softened butter
For the batter:	*For the batter:*
2 oz (50g) wholemeal flour	½ cup whole wheat flour
3 free-range eggs, beaten	3 free-range eggs, beaten
12 fl oz (350ml) milk	1½ cups milk
Sea salt	Sea salt
Freshly ground black pepper	Freshly ground black pepper
1 teaspoon raw cane sugar	1 teaspoon raw cane sugar
Freshly grated nutmeg	Freshly grated nutmeg
1 tablespoon dark rum	1 tablespoon dark rum

Boil the quince slices for 10 minutes, then drain well. Wash the aubergine (eggplant) slices under cold running water. Pat dry and coat in crushed almonds.

Heat the oil in a pan and sauté the aubergine (eggplant) slices on both sides until just softened. Drain well and reserve. In the same oil sauté the garlic and onion until softened. Drain and reserve.

Thinly slice the tomato. Grease an oblong ovenproof dish with the butter and set aside.

In a bowl, beat together the flour, eggs and milk. Season with salt, pepper, sugar and nutmeg. Pour the batter into the greased dish.

Arrange over the batter rows of quince, aubergine (eggplant), onion rings, and tomato.

Place in a preheated oven at 350°F/175°C (Gas Mark 4) and cook for 45 minutes. Remove from the oven and sprinkle with the rum. Serve hot or cold, cut crossways into slices so that everyone gets some of each of the vegetables.

GRATIN DE BROCOLI AUX GRAINES DE BLÉ VERT

Broccoli and Wheat Berry Gratin

Preparation time: 10 minutes
Cooking time: 40 minutes

Do make every effort to find fresh green wheat berries for this dish, as the flavour and texture is incomparable. But it is still very good with mature berries that need soaking in warm water for 5 or 6 hours before cooking.

Imperial (Metric)	American
2 tablespoons walnut or olive oil	2 tablespoons walnut or olive oil
1 medium onion, thinly sliced	1 medium onion, thinly sliced
2 cloves garlic, chopped	2 cloves garlic, chopped
8 oz (225g) green wheat berries	1 cup green wheat berries
½ pint (300ml) dry white wine	1⅓ cups dry white wine
½ pint (300ml) water	1⅓ cups water
8 oz (225g) scrubbed and quartered new potatoes	1¼ cups scrubbed and quartered new season potatoes
8 oz (225g) broccoli	2 cups broccoli
2 courgettes, thickly sliced	2 zucchini, thickly sliced
1 teaspoon yeast extract	1 teaspoon yeast extract
Sea salt	Sea salt
Freshly ground black pepper	Freshly ground black pepper
2 oz (50g) grated Gruyère cheese	½ cup grated Gruyère cheese

Heat the oil in a large iron skillet and sauté the onion and garlic for 2 minutes without browning. Add the wheat berries and cook for 3 more minutes, stirring the mixture well.

Add the wine and water, bring to the boil and then add the potatoes to the pan. Cut the broccoli stems from the florets and stir in the stems, reserving the florets for later. Add the sliced courgettes (zucchini) to the pan. Stir everything well, then leave to simmer for 15 minutes.

Stir in the broccoli florets and the yeast extract. Cook for 10 more minutes. Check seasoning.

By now the wheat berries will have absorbed much of the liquid, all the vegetables should be just cooked, and the remaining liquid will have become a rich and savoury sauce. Sprinkle the skillet with grated cheese and place under a hot grill (broiler) until the cheese is sizzling and browned. Serve at once, from the skillet.

Note: A sprinkling of breadcrumbs in place of the cheese makes this a delicious vegan dish.

MARRONS À LA PÉRIGOURDINE

Chestnut Fricasée

Serves: 6
Preparation time: 10 minutes
Cooking time: 15 minutes

The chestnuts of the Périgord region are the best in France. I first served this dish in 1947, at the opening of the famous Caprice restaurant.

Imperial (Metric)	American
1 lb (450g) peeled fresh chestnuts	1 pound peeled fresh chestnuts
1 lb (450g) Brussels sprouts	1 pound Brussels sprouts
8 oz (225g) swedes, diced	1½ cups diced rutabaga
2 fl oz (60ml) walnut oil	¼ cup walnut oil
1 medium onion, chopped	1 medium onion, chopped
2 sticks celery, chopped	2 stalks celery, chopped
1 teaspoon mustard seeds	1 teaspoon mustard seeds
1 small piece fresh ginger	1 small piece fresh ginger
1 small black truffle, scrubbed	1 small black truffle, scrubbed
1 tablespoon clear honey	1 tablespoon clear honey
Sea salt	Sea salt
Freshly ground black pepper	Freshly ground black pepper
Freshly grated nutmeg	Freshly grated nutmeg

Boil the chestnuts for 10 minutes. Trim the sprouts and cut in half if large, then boil for 8 minutes. Boil the swedes (rutabaga) for 5 minutes. Drain all the vegetables well.

Heat the oil in a large pan and sauté the onion and celery for 2 minutes. Add the mustard seeds, then stir in all the vegetables and cook gently to reheat thoroughly.

Chop the ginger finely, and thinly slice the truffle. Stir these into the hot vegetables along with the honey. Season to taste. Serve at once on a bed of dandelion or chicory (endive) salad.

Variations: If truffles are unavailable, or beyond your budget, substitute a large field mushroom but add it with the other vegetables so that it cooks briefly. Butter could be used instead of walnut oil and gives a good flavour.

CASSATE DE LÉGUMES ORLÉANAISE

A Three-Layer Vegetable Loaf

Serves: 8
Preparation time: 15 minutes
Cooking time: 1½ hours

The region of Joan of Arc has a rich repertoire of vegetable terrines such as this one, which is as good to eat as it is to look at.

Imperial (Metric)	American
1½ lb (675g) carrots	1½ pounds carrots
1½ lb (675g) French beans	1½ pounds snap beans
1½ lb (675g) leeks	1½ pounds leeks
8 fresh tarragon leaves	8 fresh tarragon leaves
8 chives, snipped	8 chives, snipped
1 tablespoon chopped coriander leaves	1 tablespoon chopped coriander leaves
1 teaspoon caraway seeds	1 teaspoon caraway seeds
8 oz (225g) cream cheese	1 cup cream cheese
6 free-range eggs	6 free-range eggs
Sea salt	Sea salt
Freshly ground black pepper	Freshly ground black pepper
Freshly grated nutmeg	Freshly grated nutmeg
2 oz (50g) butter	¼ cup butter

Scrub and slice the carrots. Top and tail the beans. Trim the leeks, slice into 1 inch (2.5cm) chunks and wash very well. Cook all the vegetables separately for 15 minutes each, then drain well.

In a blender, processor or food mill, purée the carrots with the tarragon and place the mixture in a bowl. Then purée the beans with the chives and place in another bowl. Last, purée the leeks with the coriander and caraway and place in a third bowl.

Beat one-third of the cheese into each mixture, then add 2 beaten eggs to each bowl and mix well. Season each mixture to taste.

Butter a large loaf tin. Place the leek purée in the base of the tin, then the carrot purée, and top with the bean purée. Place in a bain marie and bake at 400°F/200°C (Gas Mark 6) for about 1¼ hours.

Leave in the dish for 10 minutes before unmoulding onto a warmed serving platter. Garnish with baby carrots that have been flavoured with honey and ginger.

Variation: The dish could be cooked in individual ramekins which are baked in the same way, at the same temperature, but for half the time.

PAIN DE LENTILLES DU PUY, À L'AIGRE-DOUX

Lentil Loaf with Yogurt and Herbs

Serves: 6
Preparation time: 15 minutes
Cooking time: 1 hour 10 minutes

This rich, rustic loaf is a traditional recipe which may have been introduced to France by the Romans — they believed this nourishing food to induce indolence, so perhaps they hoped to quell the rebellious natives that way!

Imperial (Metric)	American
2 oz (50g) butter	$\frac{1}{4}$ cup butter
8 oz (225g) red lentils	1 cup red lentils
2 fl oz (60ml) sunflower oil	$\frac{1}{4}$ cup sunflower oil
1 medium onion, chopped	1 medium onion, chopped
2 cloves garlic, crushed	2 cloves garlic, crushed
2 teaspoons curry powder	2 teaspoons curry powder
4 tablespoons tomato purée	4 tablespoons tomato paste
$\frac{1}{4}$ pint (150ml) dry white wine	$\frac{2}{3}$ cup dry white wine
Sea salt	Sea salt
Freshly ground black pepper	Freshly ground black pepper
1 tablespoon chopped fresh basil	1 tablespoon chopped fresh basil
1 tablespoon chopped fresh coriander	1 tablespoon chopped fresh coriander
1 small green chilli, chopped	1 small green chili, chopped
2 large free-range eggs, beaten	2 large free-range eggs, beaten
3 fl oz (90ml) sour cream	$\frac{1}{3}$ cup sour cream

Use the butter to grease a large loaf tin, then place the tin in the refrigerator to harden the butter coating.

Pick over the lentils for stones or impurities, then place in a pan with double their volume of water, bring to the boil and cook for 15 minutes until softened and quite dry. Remove from the heat and place in a mixing bowl.

Heat the oil in a pan and sauté the onion and garlic for 2 minutes, to soften. Stir in the curry powder and cook briefly, then add the tomato purée (paste) and wine. Boil for 5 minutes.

Beat this mixture into the lentils, then season to taste and add the herbs and chilli.

In a small bowl, beat together the eggs and cream, then stir this mixture into the lentils.

Fill the mould with this mixture, place in a bain marie and bake at 375°F/190°C (Gas Mark 5) for 45 minutes. Let stand for 12 minutes before unmoulding. Serve hot or cold with a rice salad for a protein-balanced main meal.

POIVRONS FARÇIS AUX PIGNONS DE PINS

Peppers Stuffed with Rice and Pine Nuts (Pignoli)

Preparation time: 10 minutes
Cooking time: 45 to 50 minutes

The pine trees that yield tasty and nutritious nuts are typical of the Landes region near Bordeaux. Choose a variety of colours of pepper to make this an especially beautiful dish — you could even have one red, one green, one yellow and one black if you liked!

Imperial (Metric)	American
3 fl oz (90ml) olive oil	$\frac{1}{3}$ cup olive oil
1 onion, chopped	1 onion, chopped
4 cloves garlic, chopped	4 cloves garlic, chopped
5 oz (125g) brown rice	$\frac{3}{4}$ cup brown rice
1 teaspoon turmeric	1 teaspoon turmeric
1 teaspoon curry powder	1 teaspoon curry powder
2 tablespoons pine nuts	2 tablespoons pignoli
1 oz (25g) diced dried apricots	$\frac{1}{4}$ cup diced dried apricots
1 green chilli, seeded and sliced	1 green chili, seeded and sliced
1$\frac{1}{4}$ pints (700ml) water	3 cups water
1 unsalted vegetable stock cube	1 unsalted vegetable stock cube
Sea salt	Sea salt
Freshly ground black pepper	Freshly ground black pepper
4 peppers, of equal size, with flat bases	4 peppers, of equal size, with flat bases
$\frac{1}{2}$ pint (300ml) vegetable stock	1$\frac{1}{3}$ cups vegetable stock

Heat the olive oil in a large pan and sauté the onion and garlic for 1 minute. Stir in the rice and cook for a further minute to allow the flavours to impregnate the grains. Add the spices, nuts, fruit and chilli, then pour on the water. Crumble in the stock cube, bring the water to the boil, cover and simmer until the rice is cooked. Season lightly.

Cut away the stalk of the peppers to make an opening in their tops. Remove all the seeds and white pith. Fill the peppers with the rice mixture, then stand them in an ovenproof dish.

Pour in sufficient vegetable stock to come a little way up the sides of the peppers, then bake in a preheated oven at 425°F/220°C (Gas Mark 7) for 15 to 20 minutes. Serve hot or cold, with a tomato and basil salad.

Chapter 6
LES PLATS FARINEUX

Versatile Pasta and Pancakes

This chapter is devoted to dishes which fall neither exactly into the previous chapter, nor the one to follow. I would not class them as *plats du jour*, since one of their advantages is that much if not all preparation and cooking can be done in advance, nor are they what most people would describe as light dishes, in the sense I will adopt for the next chapter, although many will make an admirable supper, especially on a Winter's evening. So I have collected them together and placed them here, between the two, in a chapter for you to use just as you wish!

For, as you can see from the title, all the recipes in this chapter revolve around either pasta noodles of one sort or another, or pancakes (crêpes). Thus, they are usually simple to make, nourishing and substantial, relying on a base that marries flour and egg in almost every case, and teams it with a variety of sauces and fillings so wide that one can only ever make suggestions that scratch the surface of the subject. By the way, I have said that all marry flour and egg — which, if you make your own pasta from my master recipe, almost all do. I apologize to my vegan readers for this and trust they will substitute ingredients where necessary to match with the vegan sauces in this part of the book.

While everyone would agree that crêpes are a classic part of French country cooking, fewer realize the extent to which pasta is used, especially in the southern part of the country. We French love our sauces dearly, and pasta provides a perfect partner for these. I hope you will try my recipe for making your own noodles — fresh pasta is really quite special, and you could vary the flavourings to suit yourself, perhaps adding chopped fresh herbs, ground seeds, or crushed garlic.

So whether you are looking for a main meal to serve to friends, a family dish for lunch or supper, or a simple starter to prepare in advance, I feel sure you will find the dish you are looking for here.

PÂTÉ À NOUILLE À LA FRANÇAISE

French Noodle Paste

Makes: 8 portions
Preparation time: 15 minutes, plus 30 minutes resting time
Cooking time: 3–8 minutes, approximately

Pasta and noodles, so often associated just with Italy or the Orient, are just as well beloved by the French — after all, they give us the perfect base for the many sauces of which we are so fond!

Imperial (Metric)	American
14 oz (400g) wholemeal flour	3½ cups whole wheat flour
2 oz (50g) fine wholemeal semolina	½ cup fine whole wheat semolina
Sea salt	Sea salt
2 free-range eggs, beaten	2 free-range eggs, beaten
4 fl oz (120ml) water	½ cup water
1 tablespoon sunflower or olive oil	1 tablespoon sunflower or olive oil

Place the flour, semolina and a generous sprinkling of salt in a bowl or food processor. Blend in the eggs, water and oil, by hand or with the steel blades of the processor, until a smooth dough is achieved. Knead into a ball, place in an oiled polythene bag and leave to rest for 30 minutes.

Roll out thinly on a floured board and cut into ribbons of your desired width. The pasta can now be cooked straight away, very briefly, in plenty of boiling salted water, or dried in a hot oven on a baking tray sprinkled with semolina. Using the latter technique the noodles can be stored for use over the next few days, but cooking time will be extended to about 8 minutes.

Variations:
Les Nouilles Vertes Instead of using 4 fl oz (120ml/½ cup) water, blend 3 fl oz (90ml/⅓ cup) of water with 1 oz (25g/2 tablespoons) cooked spinach, so that the volume of liquid remains the same, then proceed with the recipe as above.

Les Nouilles Roses Stir together 3 fl oz (90ml/⅓ cup) of water with 2 tablespoons of tomato purée (paste), ensuring that the total liquid comes to 4 fl oz (120ml/½ cup), then proceed with the recipe as above.

Les Nouilles Jaunes Soak 6 strands saffron in the water, bring to the boil and then cool and strain before using the yellow water in the recipe as above. Alternatively, replace the two whole eggs with 4 egg yolks for a rich, naturally golden pasta.

As well as noodles, the pasta dough can be used to make lasagne, ravioli, and many other pretty and practical pasta shapes.

LAZAGNE AUX COURGES DU MIDI

Exotic Lasagne

Serves: 6
Preparation time: 12 minutes
Cooking time: 40 minutes

This dish reflects the cosmopolitan cuisine of the South of France, with its harmony of a traditional Italian pasta dish and the ingredients in common use by the Vietnamese refugees who have settled in the region.

Imperial (Metric)	American
2 lb (1 kilo) marrow	2 pounds summer squash
8 oz (225g) green noodle dough	1¼ cups green noodle dough
2 fl oz (60ml) sunflower oil	¼ cup sunflower oil
1 medium onion, chopped	1 medium onion, chopped
4 cloves garlic, chopped	4 cloves garlic, chopped
1 small piece preserved ginger, cut into strips	1 small piece preserved ginger, cut into strips
4 oz (100g) fresh pineapple, cubed	⅔ cup cubed fresh pineapple
5 oz (125g) chopped cashew nuts	1 cup chopped cashew nuts
Sea salt	Sea salt
Freshly ground black pepper	Freshly ground black pepper
8 oz (225g) firm tofu, sliced	1 cup firm tofu, sliced
3 oz (75g) peanut butter	⅔ cup peanut butter

Peel, seed and slice the marrow (squash) thinly. Bring a pan of lightly salted water to the boil and cook the slices for 6 minutes, then drain well.

Roll out the pasta dough thinly. Cut into oblong sheets about 5 × 3 inches (12 × 7cm). In another pan of boiling salted water, blanch the sheets for 4 minutes, then drain and keep them in cold water until needed.

Heat the oil in a pan and sauté the onion for 2 minutes. Stir in the garlic and cook a further 30 seconds before adding the ginger, pineapple and nuts. Cook gently for 4 minutes.

Stir in the marrow (squash) slices and season to taste. Lastly, gently stir in the tofu slices and remove the mixture from the heat.

Place a layer of filling mixture in the base of an oblong ovenproof dish. Cover with a layer of pasta, then another of filling, and finally another layer of pasta. Spread this top layer with peanut butter, thinned with a little cream if too thick.

Bake in a preheated oven at 375°F/190°C (Gas Mark 5) for 30 minutes. Serve straight from the oven.

LES NOUILLES VERTES AU CHOU

Green Pasta and Cabbage Sauté

Preparation time: 5 minutes
Cooking time: 10 minutes

This dish combines the mellow softness of noodles with the refreshing bite of lightly cooked cabbage and the delicious texture of walnuts for a simple but superb supper dish.

Imperial (Metric)	American
5 oz (125g) shredded green cabbage	1 cup shredded green cabbage
8 oz (225g) fresh green noodles	1½ cups fresh green noodles
1 medium onion, thinly sliced	1 medium onion, thinly sliced
2 fl oz (60ml) sunflower oil	¼ cup sunflower oil
Sea salt	Sea salt
Freshly ground black pepper	Freshly ground black pepper
¼ pint (150ml) natural yogurt	⅔ cup plain yogurt
2 oz (50g) chopped walnuts	½ cup chopped walnuts

Cook the shredded cabbage in lightly salted boiling water for 8 minutes.

Cook the noodles in lightly salted boiling water for about 3 minutes or until just tender.

Heat the oil in a large sauté pan and cook the onion briefly. Add the cabbage and noodles and toss to coat in the onion-flavoured oil and mingle. Season well.

Serve the mixture in 4 warmed bowls and offer yogurt and nuts for your family or guests to swirl in themselves, according to taste.

Variation: Spinach could be substituted for the cabbage, but the cooking time will be much less — just a few minutes, and with no water other than that clinging to the leaves after washing. Chop after cooking. The juice of 1 lemon, added to the spinach after cooking, improves the subtle flavour immensely.

SPAGHETTI PRINCESSE DE MONACO

Spaghetti with Spicy Ratatouille Sauce

Serves: 6
Preparation time: 15 minutes, plus 30 minutes draining time
Cooking time: 25 minutes

Pasta is popular all along the French Riviera. I have named this dish in memory of the late Princess Grace — it is beautiful, elegant and exciting, as was that charming lady.

Imperial (Metric)	American
3 small, young aubergines	3 small, young eggplants
Sea salt	Sea salt
2 fl oz (60ml) sunflower oil	$\frac{1}{4}$ cup sunflower oil
1 medium onion, thinly sliced	1 medium onion, thinly sliced
3 cloves garlic, chopped	3 cloves garlic, chopped
1 green or red pepper, thinly sliced	1 green or red pepper, thinly sliced
2 oz (50g) tomato purée	$\frac{1}{4}$ cup tomato paste
$\frac{1}{4}$ pint (150ml) water	$\frac{2}{3}$ cup water
1 teaspoon curry powder	1 teaspoon curry powder
1 teaspoon fresh chopped basil	1 teaspoon fresh chopped basil
8 oz (225g) fresh spaghetti	$1\frac{1}{2}$ cups fresh spaghetti
4 field mushrooms, cleaned and sliced	4 field mushrooms, cleaned and sliced
Freshly ground black pepper	Freshly ground black pepper
5 oz (125g) firm tofu	$\frac{2}{3}$ cup firm tofu
2 tablespoons toasted sesame seeds or flaked almonds	2 tablespoons toasted sesame seeds or slivered almonds
Fresh herbs, chopped	Fresh herbs, chopped

Cut the aubergines (eggplants) into 1 inch (2.5cm) cubes. Sprinkle with salt and leave to drain off the bitter juices for 30 minutes. Wash and drain well.

Heat most of the oil in a large pan and sauté the onion for 2 minutes, then add the garlic and cook for 1 minute more. Add the pepper and aubergines (eggplants), stir well, cover and cook gently for 10 minutes.

Stir the mixture again before adding the tomato purée (paste), water, curry powder and basil. Cook gently for a further 12 minutes.

Heat a large pan of salted water to a rolling boil. Add the spaghetti and cook until tender — about 12 minutes if dry, less if fresh.

To the ratatouille sauce mixture, add the mushrooms and seasoning.

Cut the firm tofu into small dice. Heat the remaining oil in a large sauté pan and sauté the tofu for just 30 seconds, until heated through and sizzling. Drain with a slotted spoon.

Drain the cooked spaghetti and toss briefly in the hot oil. Season to taste and swirl attractively onto 6 shallow soup plates. Over each, spoon some ratatouille sauce. Over this, neatly arrange cubes of fried tofu, then sprinkle with sesame seeds or almonds. Finally, for a special fragrance, sprinkle with chopped fresh herbs such as coriander or chervil. Serve at once.

LES RAVIOLIS À LA MÉDICI

Pasta Parcels, Stuffed with Spinach and Cheese

Serves: 6
Preparation time: 15 minutes
Cooking time: 8 minutes

Ravioli may have been introduced to France, as were so many Italian dishes, by Queen Maria de Medici. She brought her own retinue of chefs with her when she came to live there, so afraid was she of poisoning!

Imperial (Metric)	American
1 lb (450g) fresh noodle dough	2⅔ cups fresh noodle dough
A little wholemeal semolina	A little whole wheat semolina
6 oz (150g) cooked spinach	1 cup cooked spinach
4 oz (100g) cream cheese	½ cup cream cheese
2 oz (50g) grated cheese	½ cup grated cheese
2 free-range egg yolks, beaten	2 free-range egg yolks, beaten
Sea salt	Sea salt
Freshly ground black pepper	Freshly ground black pepper
1 recipe Tomato Coulis (page 80)	1 recipe Tomato Coulis (page 80)
2 oz (50g) Brie or Camembert	2 ounces Brie or Camembert

Roll out the dough on a board sprinkled with semolina. Cut two large oblongs of equal size.

Squeeze any excess water from the spinach and chop finely. In a bowl, beat together the cheeses and the egg yolks. Stir in the spinach and mix well. Season to taste.

Place spoonsful of the mixture at regular intervals along one sheet of dough, leaving enough space for a cutter to cut and seal the pasta. Wet the pastry all around the mounds of filling, then lay the other sheet of dough over the top and press down gently in the gaps between the filling. Use a ravioli cutter, or a round pastry cutter of 2 inches (5cm) diameter, to cut individual ravioli. Make sure the filling is completely sealed in. Place the ravioli on a sheet of baking paper sprinkled with semolina and leave to dry for 1 hour.

Bring a deep pan of salted water to the boil and drop the ravioli in. Bring back to the boil and cook for 8 minutes. Remove with a slotted spoon, place in cold water and leave for 1 hour.

Make the coulis as described on page 80. Five minutes before serving, place the ravioli in the sauce to reheat. Turn the pasta and sauce out into a gratin dish, garnish with slivers of Brie or Camembert and place under a hot grill (broiler) to brown lightly before serving.

LES CANNELONS DE NAPOLÉON

Savoury Rolls with Asparagus and Goat's Cheese

Preparation time: 15 minutes
Cooking time: 5 minutes

This was a dish cooked for Napoleon by his chef Laguipière, and combines the Italian influence, so strong in Napoleon's homeland of Corsica, with an aura of French gastronomy. The poor chef was just one of many who died — of frostbite — during this great leader's disastrous Russian campaign.

Imperial (Metric)	American
1 lb (450g) noodle dough	2⅔ cups noodle dough
1 oz (25g) wholemeal semolina	¼ cup whole wheat semolina
8 oz (225g) fresh goat's cheese	1 cup fresh goat's cheese
1 free-range egg yolk	1 free-range egg yolk
Sea salt	Sea salt
Freshly ground black pepper	Freshly ground black pepper
8 oz (225g) cooked asparagus	1⅓ cups cooked asparagus
2 oz (50g) wholemeal flour	½ cup whole wheat flour
2 free-range eggs, beaten	2 free-range eggs, beaten
3 oz (75g) finely crushed almonds	¾ cup finely crushed almonds
Vegetable oil, for frying	Vegetable oil, for frying

Roll out the dough on a board finely dusted with semolina. Cut into 8 oblongs, 4 × 2 inches (10 × 5cm).

Cream together the goat's cheese and the egg yolk. Season to taste.

Place a little of the cheese along the oblong in a small sausage shape. Leave some room at each edge. Press into the cheese two pieces of asparagus, cut the same length as the cheese.

Wet the edges of the pasta and roll into tubes, then pinch and fold the ends to seal in the filling completely.

Pass the *cannelons* in flour, then beaten egg, then crushed nuts.

Heat some oil in a pan and deep-fry the *cannelons* until golden all over — about 5 minutes. Serve hot or cold with dips of your choice and two salads, one green, one tomato, both with garlic dressing.

CRÊPES D'ASPERGES À LA BONNE FRANQUETTE

Asparagus Crêpes

Preparation time: 5 minutes
Cooking time: 5 minutes

In every village in Brittany you will find families cooking a variation on the traditional dish of that region — crêpes with wheat flour, buckwheat flour, rye, cornmeal, and every possible filling you can think of. Surely this simple dish is the very nicest way of using up leftovers, humble or (as here) luxurious?

Imperial (Metric)	American
4 oz (100g) wheatmeal flour	1 cup wheatmeal flour
1 free-range egg, beaten	1 free-range egg, beaten
½ pint (300ml) buttermilk	1¼ cups buttermilk
1 oz (25g) crushed toasted almonds	¼ cup crushed toasted almonds
4 oz (100g) lightly cooked asparagus tips	⅔ cup lightly cooked asparagus tips
Sea salt	Sea salt
Freshly ground black pepper	Freshly ground black pepper
Freshly grated nutmeg	Freshly grated nutmeg
Vegetable oil, for frying	Vegetable oil, for frying

In a bowl, beat together the flour and egg, then gradually add the buttermilk to form a smooth batter.

Stir in the almonds and asparagus. Season with salt, pepper and nutmeg.

Heat a little oil in a 6-inch (15cm) pan and pour in a quarter of the batter. Make four crêpes in this way, and serve, folded into quarters, on crisp lettuce leaves.

CRÉPINETTE DE POIREAUX AU CRESSON

Leek Crêpes with a Watercress Sauce

Preparation time: 10 minutes, plus 20 minutes resting time
Cooking time: 20 minutes

Watercress and leeks are a very harmonious combination. Here they provide the sauce and the filling for high-protein crêpes in a recipe from Picardy.

Imperial (Metric)	American
For the batter:	*For the batter:*
1 oz (25g) wholemeal flour	¼ cup whole wheat flour
1 oz (25g) soya flour	¼ cup soy flour
½ teaspoon baking powder	½ teaspoon baking powder
Sea salt	Sea salt
Pinch ground ginger	Pinch ground ginger
1 free-range egg, beaten	1 free-range egg, beaten
¼ pint (150ml) soya milk	⅔ cup soy milk
Vegetable oil for frying	Vegetable oil for frying
For the filling:	*For the filling:*
4 medium leeks	4 medium leeks
For the sauce:	*For the sauce:*
1 oz (25g) butter	2 tablespoons butter
1 shallot, chopped	1 shallot, chopped
1 clove garlic, crushed	1 clove garlic, crushed
3 oz (75g) silken tofu	⅓ cup silken tofu
3 fl oz (90ml) vegetable stock	⅓ cup vegetable stock
1 small bunch watercress	1 small bunch watercress
½ teaspoon Dijon mustard	½ teaspoon Dijon mustard
Sea salt	Sea salt
Freshly ground black pepper	Freshly ground black pepper

In a bowl, combine the two flours, baking powder, salt and ginger. Beat in the egg, then gradually add the milk until you have a smooth batter. Allow to rest for 20 minutes.

Meanwhile, trim the leeks, leaving as much green as possible but ensuring that all traces of grit have been washed from the insides of the leaves. Tie in a bundle and boil in salted water for 12 minutes. Drain, and press to remove all excess water.

Heat the oil in a frying pan and make four crêpes of equal size (about 6 inches/15cm). Set aside to cool.

To make the sauce, heat the oil in a pan and sauté the shallot and garlic for 3 minutes until translucent. Place in a blender with the tofu, stock, and the washed leaves from the bunch of watercress. Blend to a cream.

Return the sauce to the pan, add the mustard and seasoning, and reheat gently.

Wrap each leek in a crêpe, brush with a little oil, place on a serving plate and grill for 2 minutes until heated through. Serve with a pool of watercress sauce alongside each crêpe.

LES CRÊPES VIROFLAY AU FROMAGE DE SOYA

Spinach and Tofu Pancakes (Crêpes)

Preparation time: 10 minutes, plus 20 minutes resting time
Cooking time: 18 minutes

The original version of this pancake (crêpe) recipe was the favourite of Madame de Maintenon, who created the famous Cordon Bleu school of cookery, for the daughters of impoverished members of the aristocracy. Of course, the tofu is a modern variation, giving extra protein to this tasty dish, but it is one of which I hope Madame would approve.

Imperial (Metric)	American
For the pancakes:	*For the crêpes:*
4 oz (100g) wholemeal flour	**1 cup whole wheat flour**
1 teaspoon cornflour	**1 teaspoon cornstarch**
Sea salt	**Sea salt**
1 free-range egg, beaten	**1 free-range egg, beaten**
¼ pint (150ml) water	**⅔ cup water**
¼ pint (150ml) natural yogurt	**⅔ cup plain yogurt**
Vegetable oil for frying	**Vegetable oil for frying**
For the filling:	*For the filling:*
3 oz (75g) cooked, chopped spinach	**½ cup cooked, chopped spinach**
5 oz (125g) silken tofu	**⅔ cup silken tofu**
1 oz (25g) chopped nuts	**3 tablespoons chopped nuts**
1 clove garlic, crushed	**1 clove garlic, crushed**
Sea salt	**Sea salt**
Freshly ground black pepper	**Freshly ground black pepper**
Freshly grated nutmeg	**Freshly grated nutmeg**
1 oz (25g) butter, melted	**2 tablespoons melted butter**

Prepare the batter by stirring together the flour, starch and salt in a bowl. Beat in the egg, water and yogurt to make a smooth batter. Leave to rest for 20 minutes.

While the batter is resting, make the filling. In a bowl, blend together the spinach, tofu, nuts, garlic and seasoning.

Heat a little oil in a pan and make 8 pancakes (crêpes) of equal size. Stack on a plate lined with greaseproof (parchment) paper.

Place a little of the filling mixture into each one, and roll up. Place the filled pancakes (crêpes) in a lightly buttered ovenproof dish and brush with a little melted butter. Place under a hot grill for a minute or two until sizzling hot. Serve at once.

Note: If the pancakes (crêpes) and filling have been prepared in advance, as they can be, then a more thorough reheating will be needed. In this case, place the dish in a preheated oven at 400°F/200°C (Gas Mark 6) for 12 minutes. The dish could be sprinkled with grated cheese.

LES CRÉPILLONS CONIL

Small Pancakes with Basil, Spinach and Tomatoes

Preparation time: 6 minutes, plus 12 minutes resting time
Cooking time: 20 minutes

You will forgive me for giving another recipe combining pancakes with spinach, but I feel it demonstrates the versatility of these two foods — this dish is quite different from its predecessor, apart from being equally delicious.

Imperial (Metric)	American
For the pancakes:	*For the pancakes:*
4 oz (100g) wholemeal flour	1 cup whole wheat flour
1 oz (25g) wholemeal semolina	¼ cup whole wheat semolina
½ tablespoon baking powder	½ tablespoon baking powder
Sea salt	Sea salt
½ pint (300ml) soya milk	1⅓ cups soy milk
6 leaves basil, finely chopped	6 leaves basil, finely chopped
6 leaves fenugreek, finely chopped	6 leaves fenugreek, finely chopped
Vegetable oil, for frying	Vegetable oil, for frying
For the topping:	*For the topping:*
1 tablespoon sunflower oil	1 tablespoon sunflower oil
1 medium onion, thinly sliced	1 medium onion, thinly sliced
2 cloves garlic, chopped	2 cloves garlic, chopped
4 tomatoes, skinned, seeded and roughly chopped	4 tomatoes, skinned, seeded and roughly chopped
1 lb (450g) chopped cooked spinach	1 pound chopped cooked spinach
Sea salt	Sea salt
Freshly ground black pepper	Freshly ground black pepper
Freshly grated nutmeg	Freshly grated nutmeg
1 tablespoon toasted sesame seeds	1 tablespoon toasted sesame seeds

Place the flour, semolina, baking powder and salt in a bowl. Beat in the soya milk, basil and fenugreek. Leave to rest for 12 minutes.

Meanwhile, make the topping. Heat the oil in a pan and sauté the onion and garlic for 3 minutes. Stir in the tomato and spinach. Leave to simmer for 12 minutes, then season to taste.

Heat some oil in a large, flat pan and pour about 2 fl oz (60ml/¼ cup) of batter for each pancake. Cook until golden on both sides, then remove onto kitchen paper towels and keep warm until all the pancakes are ready.

Serve the pancakes with 2 spoonsful of topping each, and a final sprinkling of sesame seeds, but no cheese — this flavoursome dish really does not need it.

LES CRÉPILLONS CAPUCINES

Pancakes with a Mushroom and Walnut Filling

Preparation time: 10 minutes
Cooking time: 12 minutes

The dried mushrooms that have for so long been part of French cuisine are now more readily available in other countries, and are well worth seeking out for this particular recipe from the Périgord.

Imperial (Metric)	American
4 fl oz (120ml) vegetable oil	½ cup vegetable oil
1 small onion, finely chopped	1 small onion, finely chopped
8 oz (225g) dried *cèpes*, soaked, washed well and drained	1 cup dried *cèpes*, soaked, washed well and drained
4 cloves garlic, crushed	4 cloves garlic, crushed
1 oz (25g) dry wholemeal breadcrumbs	¼ cup dry whole wheat breadcrumbs
2 oz (50g) walnuts	½ cup walnuts
1 tablespoon chopped parsley	1 tablespoon chopped parsley
1 tablespoon snipped chives	1 tablespoon snipped chives
Sea salt	Sea salt
Freshly ground black pepper	Freshly ground black pepper
3 free-range eggs	3 free-range eggs
4 strands saffron, powdered	4 strands saffron, powdered
1 tablespoon natural yogurt	1 tablespoon plain yogurt
½ tablespoon wholemeal flour	½ tablespoon whole wheat flour

Heat half the oil in a pan and sauté the onion for 1 minute, then add the sliced mushrooms (*cèpes*). Cook for a further 3 minutes, stirring from time to time.

Add the garlic and cook briefly, then stir in the breadcrumbs and nuts and remove from the heat.

Mix in the herbs and seasoning, and set aside.

In a bowl, beat together the eggs, saffron, yogurt and flour. Season to taste.

Heat half of the remaining oil in a clean pan. Add half the egg mixture, scramble a little, then leave to set like a small omelette. Place half the filling in the centre, allow to warm through and then fold the pancake over and turn onto a warm dish. Keep warm while repeating with the remaining ingredients. Each pancake serves 2 people as a light meal with warm French bread.

Chapter 7
LES PLATS DE FAMILLE

Family Lunch and Supper Dishes

Like the previous chapter, this one contains a selection of wholesome and appetizing dishes for the family to sit down to together, or for you to share with good friends as an informal meal. Some dishes can be made from an impromptu selection of produce in the market, others can make delicious use of stored root vegetables, dairy foods, and dried pulses. Many are simple bakes that can be prepared in advance and transferred to the oven while you share the events of the day with family and friends, or end a busy morning with a relaxing glass of wine or cider.

As I have already mentioned, family meals are a very important part of French life, and everyone from *grandmère* to the very youngest members of the family gathers in the kitchen to help prepare the meal, lay the table, uncork the *vin de table*, chatter, share a joke, resolve an argument . . . in other words, capture just the sense of family spirit which is so often overlooked in the hustle and bustle of the modern world.

Here are dishes, then, to help recapture what, for me, is one of the most charming aspects of the French way of life. Get everyone involved in the preparation of the meal and you will add a spice and savour to your food which cannot be found in any list of ingredients!

FONDUE AUX PETITS LÉGUMES

Cheese Fondue with Fresh Spring Vegetables

Serves: 6
Preparation time: 10 minutes
Cooking time: 5 minutes

In France we like to eat our vegetables when they are young, tiny and sweet. Enormous vegetables can be consigned to the soup pot!

Imperial (Metric)	American
1 bunch spring onions	1 bunch scallions
1 small bunch radishes	1 small bunch radishes
8 oz (225g) baby carrots	2 cups baby carrots
8 oz (225g) baby turnips	2 cups baby turnips
8 oz (225g) cauliflower florets	2 cups cauliflower florets
2 heads chicory	2 heads Belgian endive
2 fl oz (60ml) sunflower oil	$\frac{1}{4}$ cup sunflower oil
1 clove garlic, crushed	1 clove garlic, crushed
8 oz (225g) grated Comté cheese	2 cups grated Comté cheese
8 oz (225g) grated Emmenthal cheese	2 cups grated Emmenthaler cheese
8 oz (225g) grated Beaufort cheese	2 cups grated Beaufort cheese
1 pint (600ml) dry white wine	$2\frac{1}{2}$ cups dry white wine
Sea salt	Sea salt
Freshly ground black pepper	Freshly ground black pepper
Freshly grated nutmeg	Freshly grated nutmeg
Bread or croûtons of choice	Bread or croûtons of choice

Wash the vegetables and drain well. Trim the spring onions (scallions) and cut into 2 inch (5cm) lengths. Trim the radishes but leave whole. Peel or scrub the carrots and turnips and cut into chunky 2 inch (5cm) sticks. Trim the cauliflower florets and break into chunks if large. Separate the leaves of chicory (endive).

Place all the vegetables in the refrigerator to crisp until required.

Heat the oil in a pan or fondue pot. Cook the garlic very briefly, then add the wine and cheese. Stir until melted and smooth. Season with salt, pepper and nutmeg. Transfer the pan to a table-top burner, or pour the mixture into individual dishes over candle-warmers. Serve a beautiful bowl of chilled vegetables to dip into the creamy mixture, along with cubes of bread or croûtons with fondue forks for dipping.

Note: If any or all of the cheeses mentioned above are hard to obtain, any hard cheese with good melting qualities would do. And, of course, you may select for your vegetables just those which are young and tender in the market that day — the list above is just a selection.

POIS CHICHES À LA CATALANE

Spicy Chick Peas

Preparation time: 15 minutes, plus overnight soaking time
Cooking time: 2½ hours

This traditional dish from the Basque region of France usually contains smoked sausages or bacon. Vegetarian and vegans can make use of delicious smoked tofu to recreate the authentic flavour of the dish — and keep calories lower.

Imperial (Metric)	American
8 oz (225g) chick peas	1 cup chick peas
1 carrot	1 carrot
1 onion	1 onion
1 stem fennel	1 stem fennel
2 fl oz (60ml) olive oil	¼ cup olive oil
2 cloves	2 cloves
4 cloves garlic, crushed	4 cloves garlic, crushed
4 oz (100g) tomato purée	½ cup tomato paste
2 to 4 green chillis, sliced	2 to 4 green chillis, sliced
1 teaspoon ground cumin	1 teaspoon ground cumin
Sea salt	Sea salt
Freshly ground black pepper	Freshly ground black pepper
4 oz (100g) smoked tofu	½ cup smoked tofu

Soak the chick peas overnight in plenty of fresh water. Drain and rinse when you wish to start cooking.

Slice the carrot, onion and fennel evenly. Heat the oil in a large cast iron pan and sauté the vegetables briefly. Add the chick peas and cloves, stir, then pour in sufficient water to completely cover the vegetables and chick peas. Bring to the boil, cover and simmer for 2½ hours, skimming off any scum as it rises.

Fifteen minutes before the end of cooking, stir in the tomato purée (paste) and chillis to taste (remove the seeds for a less fiery effect). If the mixture is still very liquid at the end of cooking, strain this off and use as a base for soups — the finished dish should be quite thick and moist but not wet.

Season the stew and stir in the cubed tofu. Cook gently to warm the tofu completely and impart a smokey flavour to the finished dish. Serve with plenty of crusty French bread, and side dishes of black olives, capers and pickled gherkins (*cornichons*) for guests to help themselves. Non-vegans could serve the dish with halved hard-boiled eggs, or a sprinkling of cheese.

BROCHETTES DE LÉGUMES HENRI IV

Vegetable Kebabs

Preparation time: 10 minutes
Cooking time: 8 minutes

King Henri IV was the first French ruler of the Bourbon line — a liberal man and a patron of agriculture and gastronomy.

Imperial (Metric)	American
1 aubergine	1 eggplant
2 fl oz (60ml) vegetable oil	¼ cup vegetable oil
Juice of 1 lemon	Juice of 1 lemon
½ red pepper	½ red pepper
½ green pepper	½ green pepper
8 baby onions	8 baby onions
8 button mushrooms	8 button mushrooms
8 fairly ripe apricots	8 fairly ripe apricots
2 tablespoons seasoned wholemeal flour	2 tablespoons seasoned whole wheat flour
2 tablespoons toasted sesame seeds	2 tablespoons toasted sesame seeds

Cut the aubergines (eggplants) into 1 inch (2.5cm) cubes and rinse well under cold running water to drain off some of the bitter juices.

Mix together in a bowl the oil and lemon juice, and brush the aubergine (eggplant) cubes with this.

Cut the peppers into 2 inch (5cm) squares, discarding seeds. Trim and peel the onions. Wipe and trim the mushrooms. Halve, stone (pit) and then quarter the apricots.

Spear these ingredients onto 4 long skewers in the order of your choice. Brush with oil and lemon, then roll briefly in seasoned flour. Place under a hot grill (broiler), and grill for about 8 minutes, turning frequently.

Just before serving, sprinkle with sesame seeds. These kebabs are very good served with an avocado or cream cheese dip.

SOUFFLÉ DE CHOU-FLEUR PICARDIE

Cauliflower Soufflé

Preparation time: 15 minutes
Cooking time: 35 to 45 minutes

Cauliflower cheese is a favourite standby dish for many people, yet if you have the ingredients for that you will almost certainly have those, too, for this very much more special and just as easy dish. To give extra protein for a vegetarian supper, I have used soya milk for the sauce, but ordinary milk could be used instead.

Imperial (Metric)	American
1 small cauliflower	1 small cauliflower
3 oz (75g) butter	⅓ cup butter
1 teaspoon mustard seeds	1 teaspoon mustard seeds
2 oz (50g) wholemeal flour	½ cup whole wheat flour
½ pint (300ml) soya milk	1⅓ cups soy milk
Sea salt	Sea salt
Freshly ground black pepper	Freshly ground black pepper
Freshly grated nutmeg	Freshly grated nutmeg
4 free-range eggs	4 free-range eggs
1 free-range egg white	1 free-range egg white
8 oz (225g) grated Gruyère cheese	2 cups grated Gruyère cheese
2 oz (50g) ground, toasted peanuts	½ cup ground, toasted almonds

Separate the cauliflower into florets. Wash well. Bring a pan of salted water to the boil and cook the cauliflower for 12 minutes, then drain and mash coarsely.

Heat two-thirds of the butter in a pan and sauté the mustard seeds briefly. Then stir in the flour to make a dry roux. Cook gently before gradually adding the milk to make a thick, smooth sauce. Season with salt, pepper and nutmeg. Remove the sauce from the heat.

Beat into the sauce one whole egg. Separate the remaining eggs and beat all the yolks into the sauce, reserving all the whites in a very clean bowl.

Grease a 2 pint (1 litre/1 quart) soufflé dish with the rest of the butter, then sprinkle with a little of the cheese.

Stir the rest of the cheese into the sauce, along with the mashed cauliflower and the peanuts.

Whisk the egg whites, along with a pinch of salt, until very stiff. Fold gradually into the sauce mixture, taking care not to beat out all the bubbles. It is better to under-mix than over.

Fill the soufflé dish with the mixture. Mark the top in a criss-cross pattern, then run the back of a spoon around the rim of the dish. This helps the soufflé rise evenly. Place the dish on a baking tray and place in a preheated oven at 400°F/200°C (Gas Mark 6) to cook for between 20 and 30 minutes. The soufflé should be risen and golden, but still slightly wobbly when moved. This gives a creamy but cooked centre to the foamy dish. Serve straight from the oven — your guests should always wait for the soufflé, not it for them!

ROULADE DE CHOUX VERTS AU FROMAGE DE SOYA

Cabbage Soufflé Roll with Tofu and Nut Stuffing

Preparation time: 10 minutes
Cooking time: 10 to 12 minutes

Here is another dish marrying classic French techniques with those of the Orient — the roulade with the stir-fry.

Imperial (Metric)	American
For the filling:	*For the filling:*
4 oz (100g) firm tofu	½ cup firm tofu
2 oz (50g) ground, toasted peanuts	½ cup ground, toasted peanuts
2 cloves garlic, crushed	2 cloves garlic, crushed
1 cooked, mashed carrot	1 cooked, mashed carrot
1 tablespoon natural soya sauce	1 tablespoon natural soy sauce
2 fl oz (60ml) walnut oil	¼ cup walnut oil
Sea salt	Sea salt
Freshly ground black pepper	Freshly ground black pepper
For the roulade:	*For the roulade:*
5 oz (150g) shredded green cabbage	1¼ cups shredded green cabbage
4 free-range egg yolks	4 free-range egg yolks
4 oz (100g) toasted flaked almonds	1 cup toasted slivered almonds
Sea salt	Sea salt
Freshly ground black pepper	Freshly ground black pepper
8 free-range egg whites	8 free-range egg whites
For the sauce:	*For the sauce:*
1 red pepper, seeded and diced	1 red pepper, seeded and diced
1 shallot, chopped	1 shallot, chopped
1 large tomato, skinned, seeded and diced	1 large tomato, skinned, seeded and diced
1 clove garlic, crushed	1 clove garlic, crushed
2 teaspoons sunflower oil	2 teaspoons sunflower oil
1 teaspoon honey	1 teaspoon honey
Sea salt	Sea salt
Freshly ground black pepper	Freshly ground black pepper

Mash together the tofu, peanuts, garlic and carrot, then beat in the soya sauce and oil to form a smooth cream. Season and set aside.

Plunge the cabbage into lightly salted boiling water and cook for 7 minutes, then drain well. Place in a food processor bowl with the egg yolks and almonds. Blend briefly, then season to taste.

Whisk the egg whites with a pinch of salt until stiff, then fold into the cabbage mixture.

Line a Swiss-roll tin (jelly roll pan) 10 × 12 inches (25 × 30cm) with silicon (parchment) paper. Fill with the cabbage mixture and level with a spatula. Bake in the centre of the oven at 400°F/200°C (Gas Mark 6) for 10 to 12 minutes, until risen and quite firm.

While the roulade is baking, make the sauce. Sauté all the vegetables in the oil until tender, then place in a blender with the honey and purée until smooth. Season and reheat.

When the roulade is cooked, remove from the oven and leave to cool for 5 minutes before turning out and spreading with the filling. Roll up carefully and leave for a few more minutes.

Place a pool of sauce on each of 4 warmed serving plates, then slice the roulade and lay slices gently onto the sauce. Serve at once.

PARMENTIER DE CHOU-FLEUR AU SAFRAN

Potato and Cauliflower Bake with Saffron Sauce

Serves: 6
Preparation time: 10 minutes
Cooking time: 40 minutes

This simple country bake makes a delicious supper, served with a jug of dry French cider.

Imperial (Metric)	American
1 lb (450g) potatoes	1 pound potatoes
1 medium cauliflower	1 medium cauliflower
2 oz (50g) butter	$\frac{1}{4}$ cup butter
2 free-range eggs, beaten	2 free-range eggs, beaten
Sea salt	Sea salt
Freshly ground black pepper	Freshly ground black pepper
1 oz (25g) wholemeal flour	$\frac{1}{4}$ cup whole wheat flour
$\frac{1}{2}$ pint (300ml) milk	$1\frac{1}{3}$ cups milk
5 strands saffron	5 strands saffron
Freshly grated nutmeg	Freshly grated nutmeg
2 oz (50g) grated cheese	$\frac{1}{2}$ cup grated cheese
2 tablespoons wholemeal breadcrumbs	2 tablespoons whole wheat breadcrumbs

Scrub and quarter the potatoes. Bring a large pan of salted water to the boil and cook the potatoes for 15 minutes.

Divide the cauliflower into florets and rinse well. Place in the pan with the potatoes and cook for a further 7 minutes. Drain the vegetables well, reserving the cooking liquid, and mash coarsely or pass through a vegetable mill.

Place the mashed vegetables in a bowl and beat in half the butter and all the beaten eggs. Season to taste, then place the mixture in an earthenware baking dish, making sure the sides are somewhat higher than the level of the vegetables.

Place the rest of the butter in a pan and melt gently. Add the flour and stir to form a roux. Gradually stir in the milk to form a thick sauce, then add about $\frac{1}{2}$ pint (300ml/$1\frac{1}{3}$ cups) of the vegetable cooking liquid to thin the sauce a little.

Stir the saffron into the sauce and cook gently to thicken the sauce and infuse the saffron. Season and strain the sauce and pour about half of it over the mashed vegetables. Keep the rest warm.

Mix together the cheese and breadcrumbs and sprinkle this over the dish. Place in the oven and bake at 400°F/200°C (Gas Mark 6) for about 10 minutes to reheat and brown. Serve at once, offering the rest of the sauce separately.

PETIT PÂTÉ DE POMMES AUX LAITUES À LA BOURBONNAISE

Little Potato and Lettuce Pies

Preparation time: 10 minutes, plus 1 hour resting time
Cooking time: 20 minutes

These delicious little puff pastry pies come from the ancient province of Bourbonnais, which was confiscated from the *Connétable de Bourbon* by François I because of his treason against the French throne.

Imperial (Metric)	American
8 oz (225g) cooked, diced potato	1⅓ cups cooked, diced potato
½ heart of lettuce, shredded	½ heart of lettuce, shredded
4 spring onions, chopped	4 scallions, chopped
3 oz (75g) crumbled blue cheese	¾ cup crumbled blue cheese
1 free-range egg, beaten	1 free-range egg, beaten
Sea salt	Sea salt
Freshly ground black pepper	Freshly ground black pepper
1 lb (450g) packet wholemeal puff pastry	1 pound package whole wheat puff pastry
Water and beaten egg, to glaze	Water and beaten egg, to glaze

In a bowl, combine the potato, lettuce, spring onions (scallions), and cheese. Beat in the egg to bind the mixture. Season to taste.

Roll out the pastry until large enough to cut 4 circles, 5 inches (12cm) in diameter. Place a quarter of the filling in the centre of each one, wet the edges, then fold over into a half-moon shape and seal the edges.

Brush the turnovers with eggwash and place on a baking tray. Leave to rest for 1 hour, before baking at 400°F/200°C (Gas Mark 6) for 20 minutes. Serve hot or cold, with salad.

GRATIN DE CITROUILLE ET CAROTTES AU MIEL

Baked Pumpkin and Carrot with Honey

Preparation time: 10 minutes
Cooking time: 40 to 45 minutes

This dish is popular in Picardy, where pumpkins grow to an enormous size. Once again, a simple farmer's dish can prove to be appetizing fare for everyone.

Imperial (Metric)	American
2 lb (900g) pumpkin	2 pounds pumpkin
8 oz (225g) cleaned, sliced carrots	2 cups cleaned, sliced carrots
8 oz (225g) diced potato	1⅓ cups diced potato
1 onion, chopped	1 onion, chopped
4oz (100g) butter	½ cup butter,
4 free-range eggs, beaten	4 free-range eggs, beaten
2 teaspoons honey	2 teaspoons honey
3 oz (75g) Gruyère cheese, grated	¾ cup grated Gruyère cheese
Sea salt	Sea salt
Freshly ground black pepper	Freshly ground black pepper
Freshly grated nutmeg	Freshly grated nutmeg
Pinch ground ginger	Pinch ground ginger
2 tablespoons wholemeal breadcrumbs	2 tablespoons whole wheat breadcrumbs
2 tablespoons crushed almonds	2 tablespoons crushed almonds

Peel the pumpkin, remove the seeds, and cut the flesh into cubes. Bring a large pan of salted water to the boil and cook the pumpkin, carrots, potato and onion for about 20 minutes until tender.

Strain the liquid off and keep as a stock for soup-making. Pass the vegetables through a mill, or mash to a firm purée.

Place the mashed vegetables in a bowl and beat in the butter, eggs, honey and cheese. Season to taste with salt, pepper, nutmeg and ginger.

Place the mixture in an earthenware ovenproof dish and level the top in patterns with a fork. Mix together the breadcrumbs and nuts and sprinkle over the dish. Bake at 400°F/200°C (Gas Mark 6) for 15 to 20 minutes, or until golden-brown.

POIREAUX AU MUSCADET

Leek and Muscadet Stew

Preparation time: 15 minutes
Cooking time: 30 minutes

This unusual dish of leeks in wine with hard-boiled eggs is well worth trying. Do not be afraid to use the spices — Muscadet wine is named for the nutmeg — *muscade* — aroma it is supposed to have, and so it harmonizes appealingly with the coriander and anis.

Imperial (Metric)	American
2 lb (900g) young leeks	2 pounds young leeks
½ pint (300ml) Muscadet wine	1¼ cups Muscadet wine
¼ pint (150ml) olive oil	⅔ cup olive oil
½ pint (300ml) water	1¼ cups water
1 tablespoon coriander seeds	1 tablespoon coriander seeds
1 tablespoon aniseeds	1 tablespoon aniseeds
1 sprig thyme	1 sprig thyme
4 free-range eggs	4 free-range eggs
Sea salt	Sea salt
Freshly ground black pepper	Freshly ground black pepper
2 lemons	2 lemons

Trim the green part of the leeks so that each is about 7 inches (18cm) long. Split the remaining green parts of the leeks so that all traces of grit can be washed away. Drain well and tie into bundles.

In a large pan, place the wine, oil, water, seeds and thyme. Bring to the boil and simmer for 10 minutes. Then add the leeks and simmer very gently, covered, for 20 minutes. In another pan, hard-boil the eggs while the leeks are cooking.

Remove the leeks and drain while you strain the liquid and season to taste. Remove and shell the eggs.

Untie the leeks and divide between 4 warmed, large shallow soup bowls. Cover with the juices. Halve the eggs and lay beside the leeks. Halve the lemons and place half at the edge of each bowl, for diners to squeeze over the dish. Serve with plenty of warm whole wheat bread with which to mop up the juices.

PETITS FLANS DE BETTERAVE SAINT VALÉRY

Individual Crunchy Vegetable Bakes with Beetroot (Beet)

Serves: 4 to 6
Preparation time: 10 minutes
Cooking time: 45 to 50 minutes

This dish uses the leaves and the root of the much-underrated beet, and introduces a tasty, crunchy flan base that can be used with all sorts of fillings to make a novel change from pastry.

Imperial (Metric)	American
For the base:	*For the base:*
1½ oz (45g) butter	3 tablespoons butter
3 oz (75g) wheat flakes	1¾ cups wheat flakes
3 oz (75g) wholemeal flour	¾ cup whole wheat flour
3 oz (75g) wholemeal breadcrumbs	1½ cups whole wheat breadcrumbs
Large pinch cumin	Large pinch cumin
1 teaspoon caraway seeds	1 teaspoon caraway seeds
4 oz (100g) vegetable margarine	½ cup vegetable margarine
Sea salt	Sea salt
Freshly ground black pepper	Freshly ground black pepper
For the filling:	*For the filling:*
6 oz (150g) silken tofu or low-fat cheese	¾ cup silken tofu or low-fat cheese
4 fl oz (120ml) natural yogurt	½ cup plain yogurt
2 free-range eggs, beaten	2 free-range eggs, beaten
6 oz (150g) chard leaves, blanched and chopped	2 cups chard leaves, blanched and chopped
1 shallot, chopped	1 shallot, chopped
4 oz (100g) cooked, grated beetroot	⅔ cup cooked, grated beet
1 stick celery, chopped	1 stalk celery, chopped
4 oz (100g) broken walnut kernels	¾ cup broken walnut kernels
Sea salt	Sea salt
Freshly ground black pepper	Freshly ground black pepper
Freshly grated nutmeg	Freshly grated nutmeg

Lightly grease 4 or 6 individual metal flan rings with butter.

In a bowl, mix together the wheat flakes, flour, breadcrumbs and spices. Rub in the margarine, season to taste, then draw the mixture together into a crumbly dough.

Press the dough into the base of the flan rings and up the sides. Bake blind for 15 minutes at 375°F/190°C (Gas Mark 5).

While the bases are baking, beat together in a bowl all the filling ingredients. Fill the part-baked flan bases with this mixture and return to the oven to cook for a further 30 to 40 minutes on the middle shelf, until the filling is browned and risen. Serve hot or cold with a green salad.

BÉRRICHON AUX OIGNONS

Fruity Onion Pudding

Serves: 4 to 6
Preparation time: 10 minutes, plus 30 minutes resting time
Cooking time: 20 minutes

This savoury batter pudding is comparable both to traditional English Yorkshire pudding and our classic French country dessert *clafoutis*. But to my mind, it is the best of the three!

Imperial (Metric)	American
2 free-range eggs, beaten	2 free-range eggs, beaten
½ pint (300ml) milk	1¼ cups milk
4 oz (100g) wholemeal flour	1 cup whole wheat flour
1 tablespoon cornflour	1 tablespoon cornstarch
Sea salt	Sea salt
Freshly ground black pepper	Freshly ground black pepper
2 fl oz (60ml) sunflower oil	¼ cup sunflower oil
2 large Spanish onions, sliced	2 large Bermuda onions, sliced
2 oz (50g) sultanas	⅓ cup golden seedless raisins
Vegetable oil, for tins	Vegetable oil, for pans

In a bowl, beat together the eggs and milk. Sift in the flour and cornflour (cornstarch), adding back any bran that is left behind. Beat together to form a smooth batter, and season well.

Leave the batter to rest for 30 minutes, while you make the filling. Heat the oil in a pan and sauté the onions very slowly until soft and golden, but not browned. Stir in the dried fruit and season to taste.

Place a teaspoon of oil in each of 4 Yorkshire pudding tins (patty pans). Place these in the oven to warm briefly. Remove them, and spoon into each 3 tablespoons of batter.

Bake at 400°F/200°C (Gas Mark 6) for 10 minutes. Then remove the pans from the oven and spoon a quarter of the onion mixture over each pudding. Cover with the remaining batter mixture.

Return the puddings to the oven and bake for a further 10 minutes, or until puffy and golden. Serve hot with a salad of chicory (endive) and lamb's lettuce.

GRATIN DE BLETTES

Cheesy Chard Cake

Serves: 4 to 6
Preparation time: 5 minutes
Cooking time: 15 minutes

Here is another dish using chard, the leaves of the beet plant. The taste is similar to spinach, although the texture is coarser and lends itself well to this rustic country dish.

Imperial (Metric)	American
1 lb (450g) chard leaves	1 pound chard leaves
1 oz (25g) butter	2 tablespoons butter
2 cloves garlic, crushed	2 cloves garlic, crushed
3 free-range eggs, beaten	3 free-range eggs, beaten
4 oz (100g) chopped walnuts	½ cup chopped walnuts
Sea salt	Sea salt
Freshly ground black pepper	Freshly ground black pepper
Freshly grated nutmeg	Freshly grated nutmeg
4 tablespoons walnut or sunflower oil	4 tablespoons walnut or sunflower oil
4 fl oz (120ml) natural yogurt	½ cup plain yogurt
4 oz (100g) grated Gruyère cheese	1 cup grated Gruyère cheese

Wash the chard leaves and shred coarsely. Melt the butter in a pan and gently simmer the leaves for about 8 minutes, until tender and most of the liquid has evaporated. Add the garlic in the last few seconds of cooking. Remove from the heat.

In a bowl, beat together the eggs and walnuts. Stir in the chard and season well.

Heat the oil in an 8-inch (20cm) omelette pan. Pour in the chard and egg mixture and cook gently, stirring at first then letting set. After 4 minutes, turn the cake carefully out onto a large, heatproof dish.

Spread the top of the cake with yogurt, then sprinkle with the cheese. Place the dish under a hot grill (broiler) and cook until the cheese is well-melted and golden-brown. Serve at once, cut into wedges.

Chapter 8
LES PLATS DE GARNITURES LÉGÈRES
Light and Delightful Accompaniments

A side dish should be an important part of any main meal, yet it is so often overlooked or relegated to a portion of chips and one of soggy, overcooked vegetables. How many people profess not to like cabbage, or cauliflower, or carrots, because they remember the unpleasant mess they were forced to eat as children because it was 'good for you'?

The new movement in vegetable cookery is not just reserved for a vegetarian diet, although I suspect that the demand for better quality and more unusual vegetables stems from the growing numbers of vegetarians who demand food which is both appetizing and original. Vast numbers of people are rediscovering the vegetables so despised in their youth, finding them tasty, full of texture, fresh and full of vitality. What a pleasure is in store for anyone who can cast off memories of the past in favour of the new cooking of the present and future!

As always, this chapter is just a sample and a starting point from which you can take ideas and recipes and make them your own. I have tried to present some familiar vegetables in unusual ways, as well as some unfamiliar ones cooked simply to allow you to sample their own flavour and character.

The second part of the chapter concentrates on that most common of vegetables, the potato. Recipes simple and exotic will, I trust, amply demonstrate the versatility of this humble root. Of course, as a Frenchman, I always appreciate the perfectly cooked and presented *frite*, but I find it very sad that this method of cooking (often very badly done) should be the epitome of the potato dish for many people, along with grey and lumpy mashed potato which has long lost all the goodness and flavour it once had.

For vegetarians especially, the accompanying vegetable dish should be a counterpoint to the main dish, perhaps providing balanced protein, perhaps contributing a different texture, flavour or colour to the plate. For this reason, just as much care and attention should be paid to this aspect of the meal, in terms of cooking and presentation. These dishes should be able to stand alone as good food, and indeed most of the recipes you will find in the pages that follow could happily be enjoyed with just a salad, a hunk of good bread and a glass of wine as a meal in themselves. The choice, as always, is yours.

LAITUES GLACÉES SAINT QUENTIN

Lettuces Glazed with a Cider Sauce

Serves: 6
Preparation time: 12 minutes
Cooking time: 20 minutes

Many members of my family have been professional caterers, some with 5-star restaurants, some with modest bistros. This dish comes from the Restaurant de la Gare at Roisel near Saint Quentin which was run by my Uncle Robert and his wife Marguerite who was one of the best cooks in our family. This light lettuce dish was her speciality, made from lettuces grown in her own large garden.

Imperial (Metric)	American
6 soft lettuces with firm hearts	6 soft lettuces with firm hearts
1oz (25g) butter	2 tablespoons butter
2 shallots, chopped	2 shallots, chopped
1 large apple, cored and sliced	1 large apple, cored and sliced
4 fl oz (120ml) dry cider	½ cup hard cider
Sea salt	Sea salt
Freshly ground black pepper	Freshly ground black pepper
4 fl oz (120ml) double cream or natural yogurt	½ cup heavy cream or plain yogurt
3 free-range egg yolks	3 free-range egg yolks

Remove any wilted leaves from the lettuces, trim and stem ends and wash well. Leave to drain.

Heat the butter in a pan and sauté the shallots for 2 minutes, then add the sliced apple and cook for a further 4 minutes. Add the cider and simmer gently for 10 minutes so that the apple is reduced to a thick purée. When the sauce is ready, set aside to cool slightly.

Meanwhile, bring a pan of salted water to the boil and cook the lettuces for 8 minutes. Drain well and squeeze gently to remove excess water. Cool slightly before folding the lettuces into neat parcels and arranging in the base of a shallow overproof dish.

Season the sauce and stir in the yogurt or cream, then beat in the egg yolks. Pour over the lettuce.

Place the dish in the oven at 475°F/240°C (Gas Mark 9) for 10 minutes to thicken and glaze the sauce. Serve at once.

CHAMPIGNONS MONTMARTRE

Simple Stuffed Mushrooms

Preparation time: 5 minutes
Cooking time: 10 to 15 minutes

The very simple stuffing for these mushrooms makes them a perfect
accompaniment to a rich stew.

Imperial (Metric)	American
8 large white mushrooms	8 large white mushrooms
4oz (100g) wholemeal breadcrumbs	2 cups whole wheat breadcrumbs
2 fl oz (60ml) natural yogurt	$\frac{1}{4}$ cup plain yogurt
2 free-range eggs, beaten	2 free-range eggs, beaten
8 leaves watercress, chopped	8 leaves watercress, chopped
4 oz (100g) grated cheese	1 cup grated cheese
Sea salt	Sea salt
Freshly ground black pepper	Freshly ground black pepper

Wash and dry the mushrooms well. Remove the stems, chop them and
place them in a bowl. Lay the caps, undersides up, in an ovenproof dish.

Stir the breadcrumbs and yogurt into the chopped stems. Add most of the
beaten egg, the chopped watercress, and half the cheese. Season well. If
the mixture is too dry, add more egg. Do not make it too runny, however.

Spoon the filling into the mushroom caps, heaping it firmly. Brush with
any remaining egg and sprinkle with the rest of the cheese.

Bake the mushroom caps at 400°F/200°C (Gas Mark 6) for 10 to 15
minutes, until golden and sizzling. Serve at once.

MÉLANGE DES ANGES D'ARMENONVILLE

Mushroom Ratatouille

Serves: 6
Preparation time: 12 minutes
Cooking time: 30 minutes

This is an unusual ratatouille which I learned while working in a restaurant in the suburbs of Paris. It is primarily made from mushrooms and aubergines (eggplants), and is cooked only briefly, unlike the traditional dish. Yet it is one of the best ratatouilles I have ever tasted.

Imperial (Metric)	American
1 lb (450g) aubergines	1 pound eggplants
2 fl oz (60ml) walnut oil	$\frac{1}{4}$ cup walnut oil
1 large onion, thinly sliced	1 large onion thinly sliced
1 lb (450g) button mushrooms	1 pound button mushrooms
$\frac{1}{4}$ pint (150ml) dry white wine	$\frac{2}{3}$ cup dry white wine
3 oz (75g) tomato purée	$\frac{1}{3}$ cup tomato paste
4 cloves garlic, crushed	4 cloves garlic, crushed
2 shallots, chopped	2 shallots, chopped
Sea salt	Sea salt
Freshly ground black pepper	Freshly ground black pepper
1 tablespoon freshly chopped basil	1 tablespoon freshly chopped basil

Thinly slice the aubergines (eggplants) and rinse well in cold running water to remove some of the bitter juices. Drain well.

Heat the oil in a large pan and sweat the onion for 4 minutes. Add the aubergine (eggplant) slices and sauté for 5 minutes until tender.

Trim and wipe the mushrooms and add to the pan with the wine. Bring to the boil and simmer for 5 minutes. Stir in the tomato purée (paste), garlic and shallots. Cover and simmer for 15 minutes.

Season the ratatouille to taste and sprinkle with chopped basil just before serving.

ENDIVE BRAISÉES, SAUCE CRESSON

Braised Chicory (Endive) in a Watercress and Radish Sauce

Preparation time: 10 minutes
Cooking time: 35 to 40 minutes

Braised chicory (endive) is a traditional dish in the Flemish-influenced regions of Northern France. In this recipe it is served with a modern watercress sauce.

Imperial (Metric)	American
For the sauce:	*For the sauce:*
2 bunches watercress	2 bunches watercress
6 radishes, cleaned and sliced	6 radishes, cleaned and sliced
1 slice preserved ginger	1 slice preserved ginger
2 fl oz (60ml) sunflower oil	¼ cup sunflower oil
8 oz (225g) silken tofu	1 cup silken tofu
Sea salt	Sea salt
Freshly ground black pepper	Freshly ground black pepper
Juice of 1 lemon	Juice of 1 lemon
For the braised chicory:	*For the braised endive:*
8 heads chicory	8 heads Belgian endive
Juice of 1 orange	Juice of 1 orange
Juice of 1 lemon	Juice of 1 lemon
1 teaspoon honey	1 teaspoon honey
Freshly ground black pepper	Freshly ground black pepper

Trim the watercress of coarse stems and leaves. Reserve a few nice sprigs for garnish and place the rest of the cress in a food processor with the radishes, ginger, oil and tofu. Blend to a smooth cream, then season and add the lemon juice. Set aside.

Trim the heads of chicory (endive), removing the discoloured end and the outer leaves. Place in a baking dish. Stir together the orange and lemon juice and the honey. Pour this over the chicory (endive).

Cover the dish with a lid or foil and bake in a preheated oven at 400°F/200°C (Gas Mark 6) for about 35 minutes. To serve, drain the chicory (endive) and place on a warmed serving dish. Drizzle the sauce over and garnish with sprigs of watercress.

Note: The heads of chicory (endive) could be browned in a little oil before braising.

153

POIREAUX CONFITS AU MIEL CÔTE D'AZUR

Leeks in a Honey Sauce

Preparation time: 10 minutes
Cooking time: 35 minutes

The perfume industry of France is centred around the little town of Grasse in Southern France, where the fields are full of lavender and other flowers. The bees there make a honey which is richly scented and flavoured with their meadow harvest.

Imperial (Metric)	American
12 small leeks	12 small leeks
2 oz (50g) butter	¼ cup butter
2 tablespoons French honey	2 tablespoons French honey
Juice of 1 lemon	Juice of 1 lemon
1 tablespoon white wine vinegar	1 tablespoon white wine vinegar
¼ pint (150ml) sweet white wine	⅔ cup sweet white wine
Sea salt	Sea salt
Freshly ground black pepper	Freshly ground black pepper

Trim and clean the leeks well. Tie them in bundles of 6 and boil in salted water for 12 minutes. Drain well and squeeze out excess moisture. Place in an ovenproof dish and set aside.

Melt the butter in a pan, stir in the honey and cook gently for about 5 minutes to make a rich caramel. Stir in the lemon juice, vinegar and wine, bring to the boil and cook for 4 more minutes. Season to taste.

Pour the sauce over the leeks, place in the oven at 400°F/200°C (Gas Mark 6) and cook for 15 minutes. Serve at once.

LES SALSIFIS COMTE DE PARIS

Salsify with Yogurt and Fresh Herbs

Serves: 6
Preparation time: 5 minutes
Cooking time: 25 minutes

Salsify is a much underrated vegetable. It really is a most pleasant and subtle vegetable, needing only a hint of shallot, herbs and yogurt to bring out its character.

Imperial (Metric)	American
2 lb (1 kilo) salsify	2 pounds salsify (oyster plant)
2 tablespoons white wine vinegar	2 tablespoons white wine vinegar
1 oz (25g) unbleached white flour	$\frac{1}{4}$ cup unbleached white flour
3 tablespoons vegetable oil	3 tablespoons vegetable oil
2 small shallots, chopped	2 small shallots, chopped
Sea salt	Sea salt
Freshly ground black pepper	Freshly ground black pepper
2 fl oz (60ml) natural yogurt	$\frac{1}{4}$ cup plain yogurt
Fresh chopped herbs, to taste	Fresh chopped herbs, to taste

Peel the salsify and wash well. Cut into quarters, lengthwise, and in half across if very long. Place in a bowl of cold water with the vinegar, to keep them white.

In a bowl, mix together the flour, 1 tablespoon of the oil and 3 tablespoons of water. This is known as a *blanc* and is used to prevent vegetables such as salsify browning during cooking.

Bring a large pan of salted water to the boil and stir in the flour paste. Add the salsify and cook gently for 20 minutes, or until tender. Drain the salsify well.

Heat the remaining oil in a pan and sauté the shallots, then add the salsify to the pan to reheat. Toss in the onion-flavoured oil. Season to taste, then spoon onto a warmed serving dish. Drizzle with yogurt, sprinkle with the chopped fresh herbs of your choice (tarragon and chervil are very good) and serve at once.

FENOUIL À LA CONFITURE DE TOMATE

Fennel and Tomato Bake

Preparation time: 5 minutes
Cooking time: 32 to 35 minutes

Fennel's pungent aniseed taste is mellowed by cooking, and is well matched in this piquant bake with tomatoes, raspberry vinegar and honey. To turn this dish into a meal, lay poached eggs over the finished dish and drizzle with a classic French *beurre blanc* sauce. Delicious!

Imperial (Metric)	American
4 large bulbs fennel	4 large bulbs fennel
1 tablespoon olive oil	1 tablespoon olive oil
4 large, ribbed tomatoes	4 large, ribbed tomatoes
1 tablespoon clear honey	1 tablespoon clear honey
1 tablespoon raspberry vinegar	1 tablespoon raspberry vinegar
4 basil leaves, chopped	4 basil leaves, chopped
Sea salt	Sea salt
Freshly ground black pepper	Freshly ground black pepper

Trim the fennel, removing any browned, damaged or wilted parts. Split each bulb down the middle and wash well. Bring a large pan of salted water to the boil and cook the fennel for 20 minutes.

Refresh the fennel in cold water, then lay in a shallow earthenware braising dish. Brush with oil.

Skin, seed and chop the tomatoes. Scatter over the fennel. Mix together the honey and vinegar and drizzle this over the dish. Sprinkle with basil, salt and pepper.

Place the dish in a hot oven at 400°F/200°C (Gas Mark 6) and bake for 12 to 15 minutes so that the tomatoes cook to a rich sauce over the fennel. Serve as described above, or as a side dish.

GÂTEAU DE POMMES DE TERRE

Potato Cake

Serves: 6
Preparation time: 5 to 10 minutes
Cooking time: 40 minutes

This wonderfully simple dish makes a pleasant change from the more usual gratin-type dishes made of sliced potato. Do not rinse the potatoes when sliced, as you would for a gratin, as the starch is needed to hold them together into their neat gâteau shape.

Imperial (Metric)	American
2 lb (900g) potatoes	2 pounds potatoes
2 oz (50g) butter or vegetable margarine	$\frac{1}{4}$ cup butter or vegetable margarine
Sea salt	Sea salt
Freshly ground black pepper	Freshly ground black pepper
Freshly grated nutmeg	Freshly grated nutmeg
1 large clove garlic, crushed	1 large clove garlic, crushed

Scrub or peel the potatoes and slice thinly. This can be done very quickly and efficiently in a food processor — if one is not available, try to cut the slices of even thickness for even cooking.

Melt the butter or margarine and brush a round 8-inch (20cm) flameproof gratin dish. Place a neat layer of potatoes in the base, brush with more fat and sprinkle with salt, pepper, nutmeg and garlic. Repeat until all the potatoes have been used up. Brush a piece of greaseproof (parchment) paper with fat and lay this over the dish.

Place the dish over a medium heat for about 4 minutes, to brown the base of the potatoes. Then transfer the dish to the oven and cook at 375°F/190°C (Gas Mark 5) for 35 minutes, or until the potatoes feel tender when prodded with a sharp knife.

To serve, remove the paper 'lid' and place a warmed serving plate over the dish. Turn smoothly upside down so that the potato cake is transferred to the plate. Serve at once, cut in wedges like a real cake.

POMMES DE TERRE AU FROMAGE DE SOYA

Creamed Potato with Bean Curd

Serves: 6
Preparation time: 15 minutes
Cooking time: 1 hour

This second recipe in our selection of potato dishes could hardly be more different from the first, and indicates the versatility of this humble vegetable.

Imperial (Metric)	American
2 lb (900g) large, floury potatoes	2 pounds large, floury potatoes
Sea salt	Sea salt
4 cloves garlic	4 cloves garlic
4 fl oz (120ml) olive oil	$\frac{1}{2}$ cup olive oil
Juice of $\frac{1}{2}$ a lemon	Juice of $\frac{1}{2}$ a lemon
6 oz (150g) silken tofu	$\frac{3}{4}$ cup silken tofu
Freshly ground black pepper	Freshly ground black pepper
2 teaspoons toasted sesame seeds	2 teaspoons toasted seasame seeds
8 stoned black olives	8 pitted black olives

Scrub the potatoes well and rub the skins with coarse sea salt. Place on a baking tray and cook for 1 hour at 425°F/220°C (Gas Mark 7).

Remove the potatoes from the oven, cut in half and scoop out the cooked pulp into a bowl. Mash until smooth.

Place the garlic, oil and lemon juice in a blender and purée until smooth. Transfer to a pan and warm through to develop the flavours.

Beat the potato purée into the pan and mix well. Then beat in the tofu to achieve a creamy smooth mixture. Season well.

Transfer the potato purée to a warm bowl and garnish with sesame seeds and olives. Serve with a hearty casserole, or as a dip for crudités, or stuff the cooked skins with the mixture.

Variation: Sweet potatoes could be used instead, for an exotic flavoured dish.

POMMES DE TERRE NOUVELLES À LA PROVENÇALE

New Potatoes with Garlic and Saffron

Serves: 6
Preparation time: 5 minutes
Cooking time: 35 minutes

This is one of my favourite recipes for new-season potatoes, redolent as it is with the aromas and flavours of Provence.

Imperial (Metric)	American
2 lb (900g) new potatoes	2 pounds new-season potatoes
1 oz (25g) butter	2 tablespoons butter
1 fl oz (30ml) olive oil	2 tablespoons olive oil
1 sprig basil	1 sprig basil
3 cloves garlic, chopped	3 cloves garlic, chopped
4 strands saffron	4 strands saffron
Sea salt	Sea salt
Freshly ground black pepper	Freshly ground black pepper

Scrub the potatoes very well. Halve or quarter if large. Heat together half the butter and oil in a flameproof dish and sauté the potatoes briefly until just starting to turn golden.

Transfer the dish to the oven and cook at 400°F/200°C (Gas Mark 6) for 30 minutes, shaking the dish occasionally so that the potatoes cook evenly all over.

Place the rest of the butter and oil in a blender with the basil, garlic and saffron. Blend until smooth.

Remove the cooked potatoes from the oven, place the pan over a low heat and stir in the garlic and saffron sauce mixture. Heat gently through, season with salt and pepper and serve at once.

RAGOÛT DE POMMES À L'ORIGAN

Potatoes with a Creamy Herbed Sauce

Serves: 6
Preparation time: 5 minutes
Cooking time: 35 minutes

This simple side dish is rich without being heavy, and piquant without swamping the food it accompanies.

Imperial (Metric)	American
2 lb (1 kilo) new potatoes	2 pounds new-season potatoes
1 oz (25g) butter	2 tablespoons butter
1 oz (25g) wholemeal flour	¼ cup whole wheat flour
¾ pint (450ml) milk	2 cups milk
1 teaspoon chopped fresh oregano	1 teaspoon chopped fresh oregano
1 teaspoon chopped fresh coriander	1 teaspoon chopped fresh coriander
Sea salt	Sea salt
Freshly ground black pepper	Freshly ground black pepper
3 tablespoons sour cream	3 tablespoons sour cream
3 fl oz (90ml) natural yogurt	⅓ cup plain yogurt
1 tablespoon chopped fresh parsley	1 tablespoon chopped fresh parsley

Wash the potatoes well and cook in plenty of boiling salted water for 20 minutes, or until tender. Drain and set aside.

Heat the butter in a large pan and add the flour, stirring to make a roux. Cook for 2 minutes without allowing to brown, then add the milk gradually to make a smooth white sauce.

Stir in the oregano and coriander, and season the sauce to taste.

Peel and thickly slice the potatoes, and stir gently into the sauce. Simmer for 3 minutes.

Just before serving, stir the sour cream and yogurt into the sauce. Spoon into a warmed serving dish and serve at once.

LES POMMES SARLADAISES

Potatoes with Truffles

Preparation time: 5 minutes, plus 10 minutes marinating time
Cooking time: 30 minutes

We end this chapter with a very special dish, combining the ubiquitous potato with the luxurious truffle. If you should be so lucky as to obtain a fresh truffle, this dish is indeed worth sampling.

Imperial (Metric)	American
4 oz (100g) fresh truffle	1 medium fresh truffle
3 tablespoons white port	3 tablespoons white port
1½ lb (650g) potatoes	1½ pounds potatoes
2½ oz (65g) butter	⅓ cup butter
2½ fl oz (75ml) vegetable oil	⅓ cup vegetable oil
Sea salt	Sea salt
Freshly ground black pepper	Freshly ground black pepper

Wash and scrub the truffle well. Thinly slice and place in a bowl. Cover with the port and leave to marinate for 10 minutes.

Scrub the potatoes. Peel if wished. Slice thinly. Heat the butter and oil together in a large frying pan, add the potatoes and sauté gently until softened and golden. After 15 minutes, add the truffle and its juices. Cook briefly.

Transfer the contents of the pan to an earthenware baking dish and level out the layers. Place in the oven at 400°F/200°C (Gas Mark 6) and bake for 15 minutes. Serve at once as a side dish or on its own with just a green salad in a simple lemon and oil dressing.

Chapter 9
LES DESSERTS DE LA MAISON
Home-made Desserts

At home, a French family meal will most often finish with fruit — a simple selection chosen from the market or the garden. Or perhaps a bunch of grapes will accompany the platter of cheeses. Certainly, the combination of sharp-sweet black grapes and a moist, fresh goat's cheese or *tranche* of farmhouse Brie is hard to beat.

A formal dessert is usually reserved for a special occasion, or at least the visit of friends or business colleagues. A Sunday lunch at home, with several branches of the family coming together to eat and talk, will often prompt a special sweet of some sort, too. But most people in France eat sweets such as are to be found in this chapter at restaurants.

That is no reason for us to overlook them here, however. For French desserts are among the finest in the world — our chefs have always made the most of the produce of lush pastures and orchards, and French family cooking has a great tradition of sweet dishes, too, using these bountiful assets. So, for the benefit of those of us who love a sweet treat to finish our meal, here is a judicious selection balancing formal and traditional, simple and exotic, rich and light.

Take care to consider other courses in the meal. If just one course has gone before, perhaps as a casual family meal, there are dishes which will amply satisfy the appetite without taxing the cook in terms of work or expense. If you have just partaken of a rich and multi-coursed dinner, common-sense will dictate a dessert which refreshes without sating the palate. For the most part, I have chosen to present dishes which can be prepared in advance and chilled until needed, or can be cooked as soon as a prior course is removed from the oven, or that need just a brief last-minute piece of attention before it can be served. I feel that if you have laboured over a main course then you should not be banished to the kitchen while conversation is flowing at your table.

Don't forget, the recipes that follow are often quite rich, and often higher than many in fat and calories. All the more reason to follow the French style, and save them for 'high days and holidays'. You can then savour them without guilt or after-effects on the digestion and waistline!

BOURDIN NORMANDE

Apple Flan, Normandy–style

Serves: 6
Preparation time: 30 minutes, plus 1 hour resting time
Cooking time: 40 minutes

This rich dessert, with its use of cream, apples and Calvados, could only come from the region of Normandy, with its lush pastures and bountiful orchards.

Imperial (Metric)	American
For the pastry:	*For the pastry:*
7 oz (200g) wholemeal flour	1¾ cups whole wheat flour
7 oz (200g) unbleached white flour	1¾ cups unbleached white flour
Pinch sea salt	Pinch sea salt
1 teaspoon mixed spice	1 teaspoon mixed spice
1 teaspoon powdered raw cane sugar	1 teaspoon powdered raw cane sugar
1 oz (25g) toasted almonds	¼ cup toasted almonds
4 oz (100g) butter	½ cup butter
4 fl oz (120ml) water	½ cup water
For the filling:	*For the filling:*
1 oz (25g) butter	2 tablespoons butter
1½ lb (700g) dessert apples	1½ pounds dessert apples
4 oz (100g) honey	⅓ cup honey
2 free-range eggs, beaten	2 free-range eggs, beaten
2 fl oz (60ml) double cream	¼ cup heavy cream
2 oz (50g) raw cane sugar	⅓ cup raw cane sugar
1 tablespoon Calvados	1 tablespoon Calvados
1 tablespoon toasted flaked almonds	1 tablespoon toasted slivered almonds

Sift the flours, salt, spice and sugar into a bowl, adding back any bran left in the sieve. Crush the almonds finely with a rolling pin and stir into the mixture. Add the butter and rub in to form a breadcrumb-like mixture. Then add water a little at a time to make a smooth dough. Roll the pastry into a ball, place in a polythene bag and refrigerate for 1 hour.

When the dough has rested, roll it out thinly. Rub the butter around a flan ring 8 inches (20cm) in diameter and line the ring with pastry, pressing it in firmly. Trim the edges.

Peel, core and thinly slice the apples and layer the pastry with this. Drizzle with the honey. Place in the oven at 425°F/220°C (Gas Mark 7) and cook for 30 minutes.

Meanwhile, beat together in a bowl the eggs, cream, sugar and Calvados. When the apples are softened and turning golden, pour this mixture over them and return the tart to the oven for about 10 minutes. The custard should be golden and set. Remove from the oven, sprinkle with almonds and serve hot or cold.

Variations: Yogurt could be used instead of cream for a slightly lighter dish. The tart could be flamed with warmed Calvados just before serving for a truly spectacular finish to your meal!

DÉLICE DE FRAMBOISE

Raspberry Mousse

Preparation time: 5 minutes, plus chilling time

Little pots of fruit mousse make a refreshing change from the more familiar rich chocolate pots at the end of a gourmet dinner, and are simple and successful for a family meal, too.

Imperial (Metric)	American
14 oz (400g) fresh raspberries	3½ cups fresh raspberries
½ pint (300ml) whipping cream	1⅓ cups whipping cream
Lemon juice	Lemon juice
Clear honey, to taste	Clear honey, to taste

Wash and drain the raspberries. Reserve 12 perfect fruits for the garnish and purée the remainder.

Whip the cream and, when stiff, fold in the puréed raspberries. Add a squeeze of lemon juice, check the flavour and add a little honey to achieve the desired balance of sweetness and sharpness.

Spoon the mousse into 4 glasses or ramekins. Chill well and serve garnished with the whole berries.

GALETTE DE POMMES ET POIRES AUX AMANDES

Apple and Pear Pie

Serves: 6
Preparation time: 25 minutes, plus 30 minutes resting time
Cooking time: 30 minutes

This next dish, also featuring apples and almonds, but combined with pears, is from Normandy's neighbouring region of Picardy.

Imperial (Metric)	American
2 apples	2 apples
2 pears	2 pears
4 oz (100g) clear honey	⅓ cup clear honey
2 oz (50g) toasted flaked almonds	½ cup toasted slivered almonds
2 tablespoons Kirsch	2 tablespoons Kirsch
12 oz (350g) packet wholemeal puff pastry	12 ounce pack whole wheat puff pastry
2 oz (50g) unsalted butter	1 free-range egg yolk
1 free-range egg yolk	

Peel, core and slice the apples and pears. Place in a bowl with the honey, crushed almonds and Kirsch. Leave to macerate for 8 minutes.

Meanwhile, roll out the pastry to ⅛ inch (5mm) thick. Cut into two 8 inch (20cm) squares or circles.

Thickly butter a baking tray before laying one piece of pastry over it. Arrange the fruit mixture carefully over the pastry, leaving a good border clear of fruit or juices.

Brush the border with water and lay the second piece of pastry over the fruit, bringing the edges together and pinching to seal tightly. Decorate the top of the pastry with lattice marks, made with the back of a knife. Brush with egg yolk to glaze.

Leave the pie to rest for 30 minutes before baking at 425°F/220°C (Gas Mark 7), on the middle shelf, for 30 minutes or until puffed and golden. Serve hot or cold, with cream.

LES FRUITS ROUGES AU FOUR

Summer Sabayon

Preparation time: 5 minutes
Cooking time: 10 minutes

The rich, ripe fruits of the Summer are dressed in a foamy and frothy sauce in this recipe, which is perfect to finish any meal in light and simple style.

Imperial (Metric)	American
6 oz (150g) raspberries	1½ cups raspberries
6 oz (150g) strawberries	1½ cups strawberries
6 oz (150g) black cherries	1½ cups black cherries
2 tablespoons Grand Marnier	2 tablespoons Grand Marnier
3 free-range egg yolks	3 free-range egg yolks
3 oz (75g) ground raw cane sugar	¼ cup ground raw cane sugar
¼ pint (150ml) sour cream	⅔ cup sour cream

Clean and hull the raspberries and strawberries, and stone (pit) the cherries. Place the fruit in a bowl with the liqueur and set aside to macerate.

In a bowl, whisk the egg yolks together with the sugar. Then place the bowl over a pan of just simmering water and continue whisking until the mixture increases in volume and thickens. This will take about 6 minutes.

Gradually whisk in the cream and continue to whisk until the mixture is like a fluffy custard. This will take about 4 minutes.

Place the fruits and liqueur in individual shallow glass bowls, reserving a few for decoration. Cover with custard and place under a hot grill (broiler) to glaze. Decorate each bowl with the reserved fruit and serve at once.

PASKAS AU COULIS DE PÊCHE DE MONTREUIL

Russian-French Peach Dessert

Preparation time: 15 minutes, plus 1 hour refrigeration time

The wonderful white peaches of Montreuil, where I spent some time before the war, still live in my memory. They are perfect for this French variation on a traditional Russian Easter dish.

Imperial (Metric)	American
3 oz (75g) softened butter	$\frac{1}{3}$ cup softened butter
3 oz (75g) powdered raw cane sugar	$\frac{1}{2}$ cup raw cane sugar, powdered
3 oz (75g) ground almonds	$\frac{3}{4}$ cup ground almonds
2 tablespoons Kirsch or brandy	2 tablespoons Kirsch or brandy
1 lb (450g) cream or curd cheese	2 cups cream or curd cheese
4 large ripe peaches	4 large ripe peaches
Juice of 1 lemon	Juice of 1 lemon
6 drops orange blossom water	6 drops orange blossom water

Beat together the butter and sugar until light and fluffy, then beat in the almonds and liqueur. Fold in the cheese until the mixture is smooth and creamy. Cover the bowl and place in the refrigerator for 1 hour.

Plunge the peaches into boiling water for 1 minute, then cut in half, remove the stones and peel away the skins. Place them in a bowl, toss with the lemon juice and orange water and leave to marinate for a few minutes.

When ready to serve, spoon the cheese mixture into the upturned peach halves, rounding the top neatly. Place two halves on each plate and serve at once.

GÂTEAU DE GRASSE AUX MARRONS GLACÉS

Chestnut and Chocolate Gâteau

Serves: 6
Preparation time: 20 minutes, plus chilling time

This rich, chilled 'cake' from Provence needs no cooking. It will keep for up to a week in the refrigerator.

Imperial (Metric)	American
7 oz (200g) unsalted butter	1 scant cup sweet butter
6 oz (200g) set honey	$\frac{1}{2}$ cup set honey
1$\frac{1}{2}$ lb (700g) unsweetened chestnut purée	2 cups unsweetened chestnut paste
14 oz (400g) bitter chocolate	14 ounces bitter chocolate
6 marrons glacés	6 marrons glacés
1 tablespoon icing sugar (optional)	1 tablespoon confectioner's sugar (optional)

Beat together the butter and honey until well mixed. Then add the chestnut paste and beat again until smooth.

Break up the chocolate and place half in a bowl over a pan of hot water to melt. When melted, stir into the chestnut mixture and blend well.

Carefully line an 8 inch (20cm) cake tin with greaseproof (parchment) paper. Pour the chestnut and chocolate mixture into this, then place in the refrigerator to set and chill.

Melt the rest of the chocolate. When liquid, pour onto a clean marble or plastic surface. When set, scrape with a palette knife to form curled shavings.

When the cake is set and chilled, turn out onto a serving platter and peel away the paper. Decorate with the preserved chestnuts (marrons glacés), the chocolate shavings and, if wished, a dusting of sugar. Serve cut into wedges like a baked cake.

MARINADE DE POIRES ET PRUNES À LA MENTHE POIVRÉE

Rich Fruit Compote

Serves: 4 to 6
Preparation time: 15 minutes, plus chilling time
Cooking time: 8 minutes

The delightful combination of fruits, briefly stewed in aromatic tea, is exquisitely refreshing on a sultry Summer's evening.

Imperial (Metric)	American
8 oz (225g) Victoria plums	8 ounces red plums
8 oz (225g) greengages	8 ounces greengages
1 lb (450g) Comice pears	1 pound dessert pears
1 lemon	1 lemon
½ pint (300ml) water	1⅓ cups water
2 oz (50g) honey	2 tablespoons honey
1 Ceylon tea bag	1 Ceylon tea bag
10 peppermint leaves	10 peppermint leaves

Peel and halve the plums and greengages, removing the stones. Peel, core and quarter the pears. Thinly slice the lemon.

Boil together the water and honey, pour over the teabag in a jug and leave to infuse for 5 minutes. Strain the tea into a large pan.

Add the fruit and the mint leaves to the pan, bring back to the boil and stew gently for 8 minutes. Leave to cool, then chill until needed.

COURONNE DE FRAISES ROMANOFF

Jellied Strawberry Crown

Preparation time: 10 minutes, plus setting and chilling time
Cooking time: 2 minutes

Agar-agar is used to set this delicious piquant jelly — the natural pectin in fresh apple juice helps, too.

Imperial (Metric)	American
4 fl oz (120ml) fresh apple juice	½ cup fresh apple juice
1 pint (600ml) fresh orange juice	2½ cups fresh orange juice
2 fl oz (60ml) fresh lemon juice	¼ cup fresh lemon juice
2 teaspoons agar-agar	2 teaspoons agar-agar
1 lb (450g) strawberries	1 pound strawberries
6 oz (175g) honey	½ cup honey
1 small cantaloupe melon	1 small cantaloupe melon
2 fl oz (60ml) Cointreau	¼ cup Cointreau

Heat all the fruit juices together in a pan. When the liquid is almost boiling, sprinkle on the agar-agar, stir in to dissolve, and boil for 2 minutes.

Clean and hull the strawberries and place in a food processor or blender bowl with the honey. Pour in half the thickened juices and blend to a smooth purée. Stir in the remaining juices.

Rinse out an 8 inch (20cm) crown mould with cold water, then pour in the strawberry mixture. Place in the refrigerator to set and chill.

While the crown is setting, halve the melon, scoop out the seeds and discard. Scoop out the flesh into small balls and place in a bowl with the Cointreau to marinade.

Before serving, turn out the strawberry crown onto a chilled serving plate and fill the centre with the mellon balls. Serve at once.

CHARTREUSE DE FRAMBOISE À LA CHANTILLY

Raspberry and Hazelnut Castle

Preparation time: 15 minutes, plus 4 hours setting time

Fresh raspberries are one of the real delights of Summer. This rich dessert is for special occasions only.

Imperial (Metric)	American
6 oz (150g) set honey	½ cup set honey
6 oz (150g) unsalted butter	¾ cup sweet butter
4 oz (100g) ground toasted hazelnuts	1 cup ground toasted hazelnuts
3 tablespoons raspberry liqueur	3 tablespoons raspberry liqueur
1 lb (450g) fresh raspberries	1 pound fresh raspberries
½ pint (300ml) double cream	1⅓ cups heavy cream
4 drops vanilla essence	4 drops vanilla essence
8 oz (225g) boudoir biscuits	8 ounces boudoir biscuits
Extra raspberries, for decoration	Extra raspberries, for decoration

Beat together the honey and butter until light and fluffy. Stir in the ground hazelnuts, then beat in the liqueur. Fold in the cleaned raspberries.

Whisk together the cream and vanilla until quite stiff. Then fold into the raspberry mixture.

Line the base of a 6-inch (15cm) straight-sided cake tin or soufflé dish with a circle of oiled greaseproof (parchment) paper. Stand the biscuits, sugared side outward, up around the side of the dish. Spoon in the raspberry mixture and level the top.

Place the dish in the refrigerator for about 4 hours until chilled and set. Turn the dessert out onto a chilled plate and peel off the paper. Decorate the top with the extra raspberries and serve at once.

GRATIN D'ORANGE ORLÉANAIS AU COINTREAU

Oranges with a Glazed Sabayon Custard

Preparation time: 10 minutes
Cooking time: about 10 minutes

This delicious orange sweet is featured at a charming inn, *Les Antiquaires*, in Orleans. It is one of my very favourites.

Imperial (Metric)	American
4 large seedless oranges	4 large seedless oranges
4 oz (100g) raw cane sugar, finely ground	$\frac{2}{3}$ cup raw cane sugar, finely ground
4 free-range egg yolks	4 free-range egg yolks
$\frac{1}{4}$ pint (150ml) orange juice	$\frac{1}{3}$ cup orange juice
2 fl oz (60ml) Cointreau	$\frac{1}{4}$ cup Cointreau

Peel and thinly slice the oranges, and arrange in a flower-like pattern on 4 chilled plates. Keep in the refrigerator until needed.

Set a large bowl, preferably a stainless steel one, over a pan of simmering water. Beat together the sugar and egg yolks in this, until the mixture lightens and thickens to form a thin ribbon when the whisk is lifted.

Into this mixture whisk the orange juice and Cointreau and continue to beat, forming a light and fluffy custard. Drizzle this over the oranges.

Place the plates under a hot grill (broiler) for about 3 minutes to glaze and lightly brown the sauce. Serve at once.

CRÉMETS AU COULIS DE FRAISE

Cream Cheese Mousses with Strawberry Sauce

Preparation time: 10 minutes, plus 10 to 20 minutes chilling time

Here is one of Normandy's best-known desserts. If you can obtain true French *fromage blanc* for this dish, so much the better. But cream cheese will certainly make a delicious dessert — albeit much higher in calories!

Imperial (Metric)	American
4oz (100g) fresh strawberries	1 cup fresh strawberries
1 oz (25g) raw cane sugar	2 tablespoons raw cane sugar
Juice of $\frac{1}{4}$ lemon	Juice of $\frac{1}{4}$ lemon
2 oz (50g) cream cheese	$\frac{1}{4}$ cup cream cheese
2 fl oz (60ml) double cream	$\frac{1}{4}$ cup heavy cream
1$\frac{1}{2}$ oz (40g) powdered raw cane sugar	3 tablespoons powdered raw cane sugar
1 free-range egg white	1 free-range egg white
Pinch sea salt	Pinch sea salt
Wild strawberries, to garnish	Wild strawberries, to garnish

Place the cleaned strawberries in a blender or processor with the raw sugar and lemon juice. Blend to a thick sauce. Chill for 20 minutes.

In a bowl, beat together the cheese and cream. Stir in two-thirds of the powdered sugar.

In another bowl, whisk the egg white with a pinch of salt until stiff peaks are formed. Gradually whisk in the rest of the sugar. Fold this mixture into the cream cheese.

Spoon the mixture into 4 moulds with drainage (either special heart-shaped moulds with holes in the base, or you can punch holes in yogurt pots and use these). Place the moulds in the refrigerator for 20 minutes (or the freezer for 10 minutes) to chill and drain.

To serve, spoon a little of the strawberry coulis onto 4 chilled plates, then unmould a cheese mousse over each. Decorate with cleaned tiny wild strawberries, or slices of normal strawberries if these are the only variety available. Serve at once.

Note: If you line any variety of mould with clean muslin it will prove much easier to unmould. Don't forget to place a pan of some sort under the draining moulds to catch the drips!

ROULADE AU MIEL À L'ESSENCE DE ROSE

Honey-Nut Croquettes with Rose Water

Serves: 6
Preparation time: 10 minutes, plus chilling time
Cooking time: 5 minutes

Rich sweetmeats of this sort, sold by the street vendors of Marseilles, are great favourites — especially with children.

Imperial (Metric)	American
8oz (225g) couscous	2 cups couscous
2 oz (50g) butter	¼ cup butter
2 tablespoons rose water	2 tablespoons rose water
2 tablespoons brandy	2 tablespoons brandy
2 oz (50g) ground almonds	½ cup ground almonds
2 oz (50g) chopped dried apricots	½ cup chopped dried apricots
2 oz (50g) honey	4 tablespoons honey
1½ oz (35g) shelled pistachio nuts	⅓ cup shelled pistachio nuts
½ teaspoon ground cinnamon	½ teaspoon ground cinnamon
2 tablespoons lemon juice	2 tablespoons lemon juice
4 tablespoons walnut oil	4 tablespoons walnut oil

Place the couscous in a bowl and rub in the butter, then stir in the rose water and brandy to form a dough. Roll this out on a sheet of greaseproof (parchment) paper to an oblong 8 by 4 inches (20 × 10cm).

In a bowl, stir together the ground almonds, chopped apricots, honey, pistachio nuts, cinnamon and lemon juice. Place in a blender and mince to a thick paste. Spread this over the couscous dough.

Starting with the longer side, roll up the dough to form a tight sausage shape. Cut this into diagonal pieces, about ¾ inch (2cm) long. Chill these for 25 minutes, or freeze for 10 minutes, to firm the roulades.

Heat the walnut oil in a pan and sauté the roulades until golden — about 5 minutes. Drain on kitchen paper towels and serve.

Note: Traditionally, such sweets are drenched in a sweet sauce before serving. If you wish to try this, heat 5 tablespoons of clear honey and 1 tablespoon Cointreau together and pour over the freshly cooked roulades before serving. A sprinkling of poppy seeds, or toasted sesame seeds, is good, too.

Chapter 10
LES BISCUITS FRANÇAIS

Traditional Cookies, Biscuits and Bars

In earlier chapters we have discovered many recipes that can make a tasty, nourishing meal, quick and easy to prepare in advance, easy to eat away from home or on the move, providing good fast food. And of course, not all these foods need be savoury. A wholesome diet doesn't mean we have to deny ourselves a sweet treat once in a while, especially if that treat can take the form of a satisfying bite of goodness, with a basis of wholemeal flour, oats or nuts to provide slowly digested carbohydrate rather than the quick rush of a sugar 'high' that leaves low-blood sugar and depression in its wake. Honey, too, can provide concentrated sweetness — you need much less of it than, say, white sugar, to flavour and sweeten a wholefood biscuit. And dried fruit can add flavour, sweetness and fibre to your fast food dessert.

Beware, though, of thinking that because these treats are wholesome they can be indulged in to excess. You will probably find that, because of all the fibre they contain, you will feel satisfied more quickly than by eating a chocolate bar. But if not (and these bars, biscuits and cookies are quite delicious) you will still take in more calories than your body needs and lay them down as fat.

One bar or biscuit in your lunch box, along with a snack from a previous chapter, will be more than sufficient to give you extra protein, energy, vitamins, minerals and fibre. And the psychological value of giving yourself a 'treat' should not be underestimated. Never let it be said I preach a life of self-denial — that is not what *French Vegetarian Cooking* is all about!

LES ROCHERS À LA NOIX DE COCO

Coconut Cookies

Makes: 20 cookies
Preparation time: 15 minutes
Cooking time: 5 to 7 minutes

These delicious little biscuit-cakes were a great favourite of mine when I was serving my pastry-making apprenticeship in one of my father's restaurants — a favourite both to make and to eat!

Imperial (Metric)	American
1 oz (25g) vegetable margarine	2 tablespoons vegetable margarine
3 free-range eggs	3 free-range eggs
8 oz (225g) raw cane sugar, finely ground	1⅓ cups raw cane sugar, finely ground
1 tablespoon dark rum	1 tablespoon dark rum
8 oz (225g) wholemeal flour	2 cups whole wheat flour
1 oz (25g) desiccated coconut	⅓ cup desiccated coconut
Pinch sea salt	Pinch sea salt

Grease 20 dariole moulds with the margarine, and press a little paper case into each one. This will ensure that the cookies keep their shape.

In a bowl, whisk together the eggs, sugar and rum. This will take about 6 minutes, as the mixture must be very light and fluffy, and the sugar must have dissolved completely.

Gradually fold in the flour, coconut and salt, taking care not to beat but ensuring that the ingredients are thoroughly mixed.

Spoon the mixture into the paper cases, filling to about two-thirds in each one. Place the moulds on a rack and bake in a preheated oven at 400°F/200°C (Gas Mark 6) for between 5 and 7 minutes. The cookies should be well-risen and golden. Allow to cool before serving.

LES BISCUITS AU MIEL DE NIORT

Honey Biscuits from Niort

Makes: 20 biscuits
Preparation time: 15 minutes, plus cooling time
Cooking time: 15 to 20 minutes

Niort, in the region of Poitou-Charentes, is 'twinned' with Wellingborough — home of the British publishers of this book! The spirit of *entente cordiale* which the idea of twin towns engenders is very dear to me, linking as it does the country of my birth and the one that I have made my home.

Imperial (Metric)	*American*
5 oz (125g) butter	Scant ¾ cup butter
4 oz (100g) honey	⅓ cup honey
8 oz (225g) wholemeal flour	2 cups whole wheat flour
1 teaspoon aniseeds	1 teaspoon aniseeds
1 free-range egg, beaten	1 free-range egg, beaten
½ teaspoon bicarbonate of soda	½ teaspoon baking soda
2 tablespoons warm milk	2 tablespoons warm milk

Place the butter and honey in a pan and melt gently together.

Place the flour and aniseeds in a bowl, then gradually stir in the melted butter and honey mixture, mixing to form a dough.

Add the beaten egg to the bowl and mix in, then dissolve the soda in the warm milk and add this to the bowl. Stir and then knead to form a smooth, firm paste. Leave to cool.

Form the cooled dough into a large sausage shape, about 2 inches (5cm) in diameter. Cut diagonally into about 20 slices of equal thickness.

Place the honey rounds on a greased baking tray. Bake on the top shelf of a preheated oven at 350°F/180°C (Gas Mark 4) for 15 to 20 minutes. Cool on a rack before serving.

LES CROUSTILLANTS DE PICARDIE AUX POMMES

Oat and Apple Turnovers

Makes: 8 turnovers
Preparation time: 20 minutes, plus 30 minutes chilling time
Cooking time: 15 to 20 minutes

These plump, crispy turnovers reveal a mouthwatering surprise of apple when you bite into them. Serve them warm for a teatime treat.

Imperial (Metric)	American
5 oz (125g) softened butter	Scant ¾ cup softened butter
10 oz (300g) Demarara sugar	1⅓ cups Demarara sugar
2 free-range eggs, beaten	2 free-range eggs, beaten
2 teaspoons bicarbonate of soda	2 teaspoons baking soda
3 tablespoons warm milk	3 tablespoons warm milk
1 teaspoon rum or brandy	1 teaspoon rum or brandy
Pinch sea salt	Pinch sea salt
1 teaspoon mixed spices	1 teaspoon mixed spices
¼ teaspoon ground ginger	¼ teaspoon ground ginger
1 lb (450g) wholemeal flour	4 cups whole wheat flour
5 oz (125g) rolled oats	1¼ cups rolled oats
4 dessert apples	4 dessert apples
Egg wash	Egg wash

Cream together the butter and sugar until light and fluffy, then gradually beat in the eggs. Dissolve the soda in the milk and beat this in, too, along with the rum or brandy.

Gradually mix in the salt and spices, the flour and the rolled oats, to form a stiff dough. Roll into a ball, cover and refrigerate for 30 minutes.

Peel, core and slice the apples.

Roll out the dough on a floured board to a depth of ¼ inch (5mm). Cut 8 circles, 4 inches (10cm) in diameter.

Lay apple slices on the circles. Brush the edges of the dough with water and fold over to form half-moons, gently pressing out excess air before sealing the apples in tightly. Crimp the edges with the prongs of a fork.

Place the turnovers on a greased baking sheet and brush with egg wash. Bake for 15 to 20 minutes at 400°F/200°C (Gas Mark 6) or until golden and crisp. Serve warm or cold, but not too hot as the apple might burn your mouth.

Note: Ripe pears may be substituted for the apples.

LES SABLÉS DE CAEN

Normandy Shortbreads

Makes: 12 shortbreads
Preparation time: 5 minutes, plus 1 hour chilling time
Cooking time: 15 minutes

Normandy butter is justly famous, and these light and delicate little shortbreads owe their reputation to this — but they taste just as good with any high-quality unsalted (sweet) butter, as you are sure to discover.

Imperial (Metric)	*American*
5 oz (150g) softened unsalted butter	Scant $\frac{3}{4}$ cup softened sweet butter
3 oz (75g) powdered raw cane sugar	$\frac{1}{2}$ cup raw cane sugar, powdered
4 hard-boiled free-range egg yolks	4 hard-cooked free-range egg yolks
8 oz (225g) wholemeal flour	2 cups whole wheat flour
Grated rind of 1 orange	Grated rind of 1 orange
Juice of 1 lemon	Juice of 1 lemon
2 tablespoons milk	2 tablespoons milk

Beat together the butter and sugar (which must be very well powdered) until light and fluffy. Sieve the egg yolks and beat them into the mixture, sift in the flour, beating, then stir in the orange rind and lemon juice. Roll the dough into a ball and refrigerate for 1 hour.

Roll out the dough on a floured board, to a thickness of $\frac{1}{4}$ inch (5mm) and cut 4 circles, 6 inches (15cm) in diameter. Mark each circle lightly into quarters with the back of a knife. Brush with a little milk.

Lay the circles on a greased baking sheet and bake at 400°F/200°C (Gas Mark 6) for about 15 minutes, taking care not to overcook. Leave to cool before breaking into quarters and serving.

LES GAUFRES DE LILLE

Flemish Waffles

Makes: 12 waffles
Preparation time: 10 minutes, plus 30 minutes fermenting time
Cooking time: 5 minutes for each waffle

True French waffles are made in beautifully decorated irons, many of which have been handed down through generations of the family. But the recipe tastes equally good coming freshly-cooked from the usual, gridded version more familiar outside France.

Imperial (Metric)	American
½ oz (8g) fresh yeast	1 heaped tablespoon fresh yeast
¼ pint (150ml) warm milk	⅔ cup warm milk
10 oz (300g) wholemeal flour	2½ cups whole wheat flour
½ teaspoon sea salt	½ teaspoon sea salt
2 free-range eggs, beaten	2 free-range eggs, beaten
1 teaspoon ground raw cane sugar	1 teaspoon ground raw cane sugar

In a cup, mix the yeast with the warm milk.

In a bowl, mix together the flour and salt. Make a well and pour in the beaten eggs, add the yeast mixture and sugar and beat everything well to form a smooth batter. Leave to ferment for 30 minutes then beat again.

Lightly grease a waffle iron and then heat well. Pour a little of the batter in — about 2 fl oz (60ml/¼ cup) per waffle — close the iron and cook, for about 5 minutes. Keep warm while the other waffles are cooked. Serve hot, drizzled with a little clear honey.

LES PETITS GÂTEAUX À L'ABRICOT

Apricot Scones

Makes: 8 scones
Preparation time: 10 minutes, plus 10 minutes resting time
Cooking time: 8 to 10 minutes

These tasty scones are simple enough to be made by children as their very own contribution to the family meal.

Imperial (Metric)	American
1 lb (450g) wholemeal flour	4 cups whole wheat flour
1 oz (25g) baking powder	1 tablespoon baking powder
Pinch sea salt	Pinch sea salt
2 oz (50g) butter	$\frac{1}{4}$ cup butter
1 free-range egg, beaten	1 free-range egg, beaten
8 fl oz (240ml) sour cream	1 cup sour cream
2 oz (50g) raw sugar apricot jam	2 tablespoons raw sugar apricot jam
Milk or egg wash	Milk or egg wash

Mix together the flour, baking powder and salt in a bowl. Rub in the butter with your fingertips.

Beat together the egg, cream and jam until well mixed. Stir this into the flour mixture to form a soft dough.

Form the dough into a sausage shape about 2 inches (5cm) in diameter and cut into slices $\frac{1}{2}$ inch (1.25cm) thick. Lay these on a greased baking sheet and brush with milk or egg wash. Leave to rest for 10 minutes.

Bake the scones in a preheated oven on the middle shelf, at 430°F/225°C (Gas Mark 7), for 8 to 10 minutes. Cool slightly on a rack before serving.

LES BISCUITS DE CRÉCY AUX ÉPICES

Spice and Honey Bars

Makes: 16 bars
Preparation time: 10 minutes
Cooking time: 30 to 35 minutes

This recipe from the Flemish region of France demonstrates the true use of the word biscuit, *bis cuit* — meaning twice cooked.

Imperial (Metric)	American
1 lb (450g) wholemeal flour	4 cups whole wheat flour
2 oz (50g) ground almonds	$\frac{1}{2}$ cup ground almonds
1 teaspoon ground ginger	1 teaspoon ground ginger
1 teaspoon mixed spice	1 teaspoon mixed spice
1 teaspoon aniseeds	1 teaspoon aniseeds
8 oz (225g) butter or vegetable margarine	1 cup butter or vegetable margarine
8 oz (225g) warmed honey	$\frac{2}{3}$ cup warmed honey
$\frac{1}{2}$ teaspoon bicarbonate of soda	$\frac{1}{2}$ teaspoon baking soda
2 tablespoons warmed milk or water	2 tablespoons warmed milk or water

Stir together in a bowl the flour, almonds and spices. Rub in the fat with your fingertips.

Stir in the warmed honey. Dissolve the soda in the milk or water and add this too. Mix well together to form a rich, pourable dough.

Pour the dough into a greased baking tin, 15 by 8 inches (38 × 20cm) and 2 inches (5cm) deep. Bake at 400°F/200°C (Gas Mark 6) for 15 to 20 minutes, until starting to turn golden.

Remove the tin from the oven and cut the dough into 16 bars, without removing from the tin. Return to the oven and continue cooking for a further 15 minutes. Allow to cool in the tin before removing and separating the bars.

LES GÂTEAUX POUR DIABÉTIQUES

Diabetic Cakes

Makes: 20 cakes
Preparation time: 5 minutes
Cooking time: 30 minutes

These sugarless cakes are rich and satisfying for everyone, but dieters should beware — diabetic does not necessarily mean low-calorie, and these tasty treats should be enjoyed in small quantities!

Imperial (Metric)	American
1 lb (450g) soft farm butter	2 cups soft farm butter
8 free-range eggs, beaten	8 free-range eggs, beaten
8 oz (225g) ground almonds	2 cups ground almonds
4 oz (100g) high-gluten wholemeal flour	1 cup high-gluten whole wheat flour

Cream the butter in a bowl until light and fluffy. Then add beaten egg and almonds alternately, a little at a time to prevent curdling.

Sift in the flour last of all, adding back any bran left in the sieve.

Spread the dough into an oblong or square $\frac{1}{2}$ inch (1.25cm) thick on a greased baking sheet. Bake for 30 minutes at 400°F/200°C (Gas Mark 6). Cut into fingers when cold.

LES CRAQUELINS DE SAINT QUENTIN

Semi-sweet Butter Crackers

Makes: 18 biscuits
Preparation time: 5 minutes, plus 2 hours chilling time
Cooking time: 11 to 13 minutes

This is an old French recipe, dating from the days of *Jeanne d'Arc*, the Maid of Orleans. These crisp little crackers are as simple as they are delicious.

Imperial (Metric)	American
4 oz (100g) butter	½ cup butter
8 oz (225g) wholemeal flour	2 cups whole wheat flour
2 free-range eggs yolks	2 free-range egg yolks
4 fl oz (120ml) milk	½ cup milk
A good pinch of sea salt	A good pinch of sea salt
Egg wash	Egg wash
1 oz (25g) raw cane sugar	2 tablespoons raw cane sugar

Cream together the butter and flour, then beat in the egg yolks, milk and salt. Cover the dough and refrigerate for 2 hours.

Dust a board with flour and roll out the dough to a thickness of ⅙ inch (4mm). Use a pastry cutter to cut circles 2 inches (5cm) in diameter.

Dust a greased baking sheet with flour and lay the circles on it. Brush with egg wash and bake at 450°F/230°C (Gas Mark 8) for 8 to 10 minutes, or until golden.

Remove the tray from the oven and brush the crackers with egg wash again, then sprinkle with sugar. Return to the oven for a further 3 minutes. Cool on a rack before serving.

TRANCHE DE FLOCON D'AVOINE AUX DATTES

Date and Oat Slice

Makes: 24 slices
Preparation time: 10 minutes
Cooking time: 20 to 25 minutes

Wholesome bars of crunchy, chewy goodness are very fashionable these days, but this recipe was made for us children by my grandmother when I was just a little boy.

Imperial (Metric)	American
1 lb (450g) dried, pitted dates	2¼ cups dried, pitted dates
¼ pint (150ml) water	⅔ cup water
5 oz (150g) cream cheese or silken tofu	Scant ¾ cup cream cheese or silken tofu
8 oz (225g) honey	⅔ cup honey
Pinch sea salt	Pinch sea salt
12 oz (350g) wholemeal flour	3 cups whole wheat flour
6 oz (150g) rolled oats	1½ cups rolled oats
1 level teaspoon bicarbonate of soda	1 level teaspoon baking soda
2 tablespoons warm water	2 tablespoons warm water
8 oz (225g) chopped mixed nuts	1½ cups chopped mixed nuts

Chop the dates roughly and place in a pan with the water. Bring to the boil and simmer until a thick, jammy paste is achieved. Set aside to cool.

In a bowl, beat together the cheese or tofu and honey with a pinch of salt. Gradually fold in the flour and oats. Mix the soda with the water and stir this into the mixture. Finally, stir in the nuts and gather the mixture into a dough, reserving a quarter in crumbly form.

Lightly oil a baking tin 9 by 13 inches (23 × 33cm) and press the dough in, levelling it out with your fingers. Spread the date paste over this. Then sprinkle the remaining crumble mixture over the top, pressing down very lightly.

Place the tray in a preheated oven at 375°F/190°C (Gas Mark 5) and bake for 20 to 25 minutes. Cut into slices when cold.

Note: For crunchier slices, use 8 oz (225g/1⅓ cups) raw cane sugar instead of honey.

CIGARETTES PARISIENNES

Rolled Biscuits

Makes: About 50 biscuits
Preparation time: 10 minutes
Cooking time: 6 to 8 minutes

Don't worry — I am not advocating cooking with *Gauloises*! Parisian cigarettes in this context are delicate *langue de chat* biscuits, rolled while still warm. They can be shaped in other ways, too, for example a fluted cup shape can then be used to hold a scoop of sorbet for a charming dinner party dessert. This recipe calls for icing (confectioner's) sugar, which is not a wholefood, but these biscuits are consumed in small quantities for special occasions, so I think we can make an allowance to achieve the correct texture and flavour.

Imperial (Metric)	American
6 oz (150g) softened butter	$\frac{3}{4}$ cup softened butter
5 oz (125g) icing sugar	Scant $\frac{3}{4}$ cup confectioner's sugar
6 free-range egg whites	6 free-range egg whites
2 oz (50g) ground raw cane sugar	$\frac{1}{3}$ cup ground raw cane sugar
4 oz (100g) wholemeal flour	1 cup whole wheat flour
$\frac{1}{4}$ pint (150ml) single cream	$\frac{2}{3}$ cup light cream

Cream together the butter and icing (confectioner's) sugar until light and fluffy.

In another bowl, whisk the egg whites until stiff, then fold in the ground raw sugar and whisk again. Fold into the butter mixture, then fold in the flour and cream to form a light, smooth batter.

Fit a piping bag with a small plain nozzle and pipe dots of batter onto a greased and floured baking sheet. Leave about 1½ inches (4cm) between dots, as the mixture will spread while cooking.

Bake in a preheated oven at 425°F/220°C (Gas Mark 7) for 6 to 8 minutes, until golden with lightly browned edges.

Shape the biscuits into cigarette-shapes around the handle of a wooden spoon — or into whatever shape you require — as soon as you can handle them. Or leave flat, if you prefer. They will firm and crisp as they cool.

Index

189